Dog Days

The art of the dog

Paula Jeffery

ISBN-13: 978-1546370352
ISBN-10: 1546370358

Author's website
www.paulajeffery.com

Dedicated to my patient husband, Graham for his unending love and support and all my dog loving family and friends for letting me draw their dogs.

I began drawing dogs in March 2017 as a result of a project challenge to produce images that a charity could either use to raise awareness or create physical products such as greetings cards, calendars, etc. My chosen charity was a Dog Rescue Centre. I posted the images on Facebook and it just grew from there. I used reference photos from Pixabay, Unsplash and Sktchy and then moved on to photos of dogs that belong to friends and family.

I've included the name of the dog and owners of those that I know.

It was a really fun project and who knows what will come next. Cats?

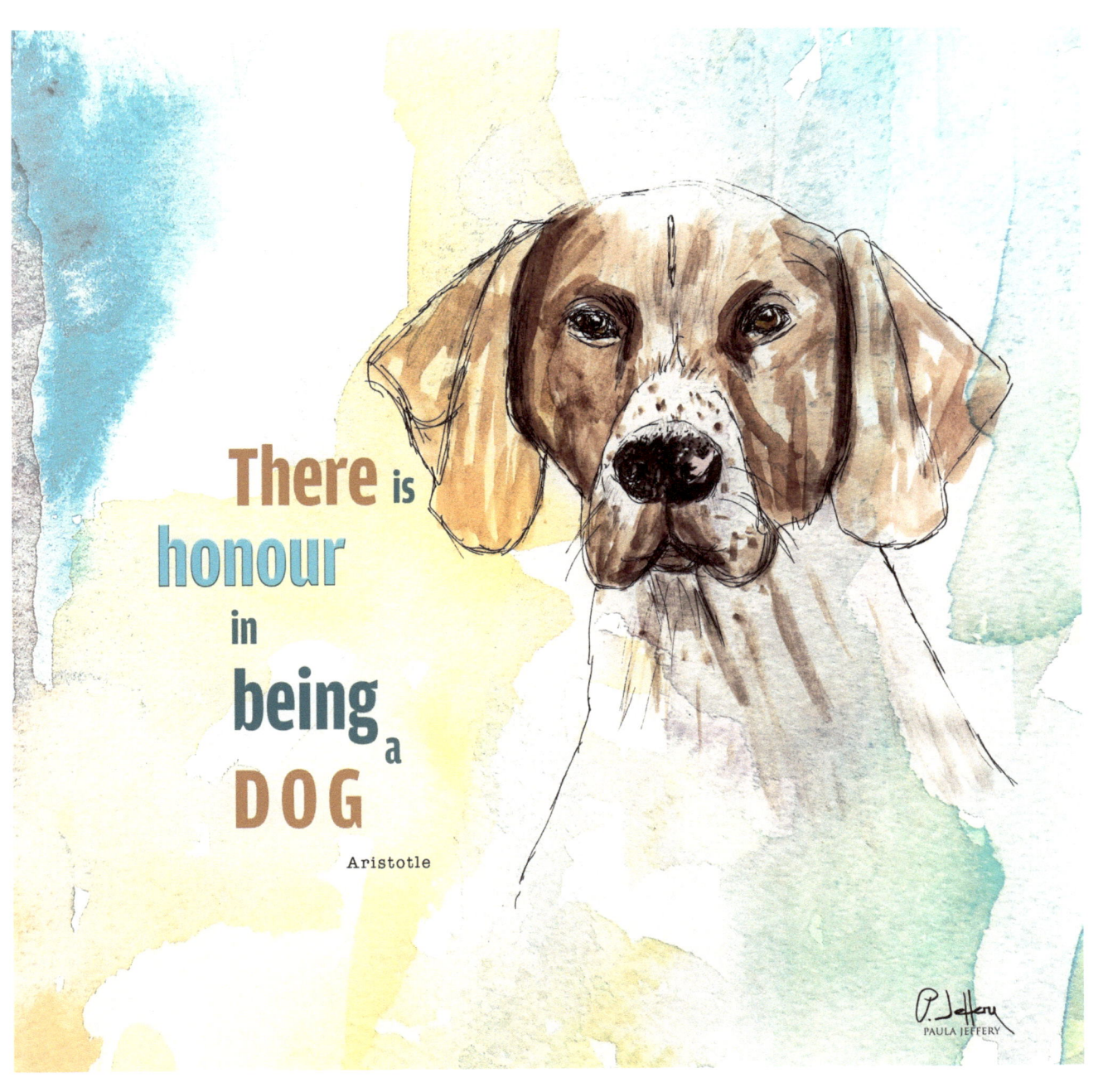

There is honour in being a DOG

Aristotle

P. Jeffery
PAULA JEFFERY

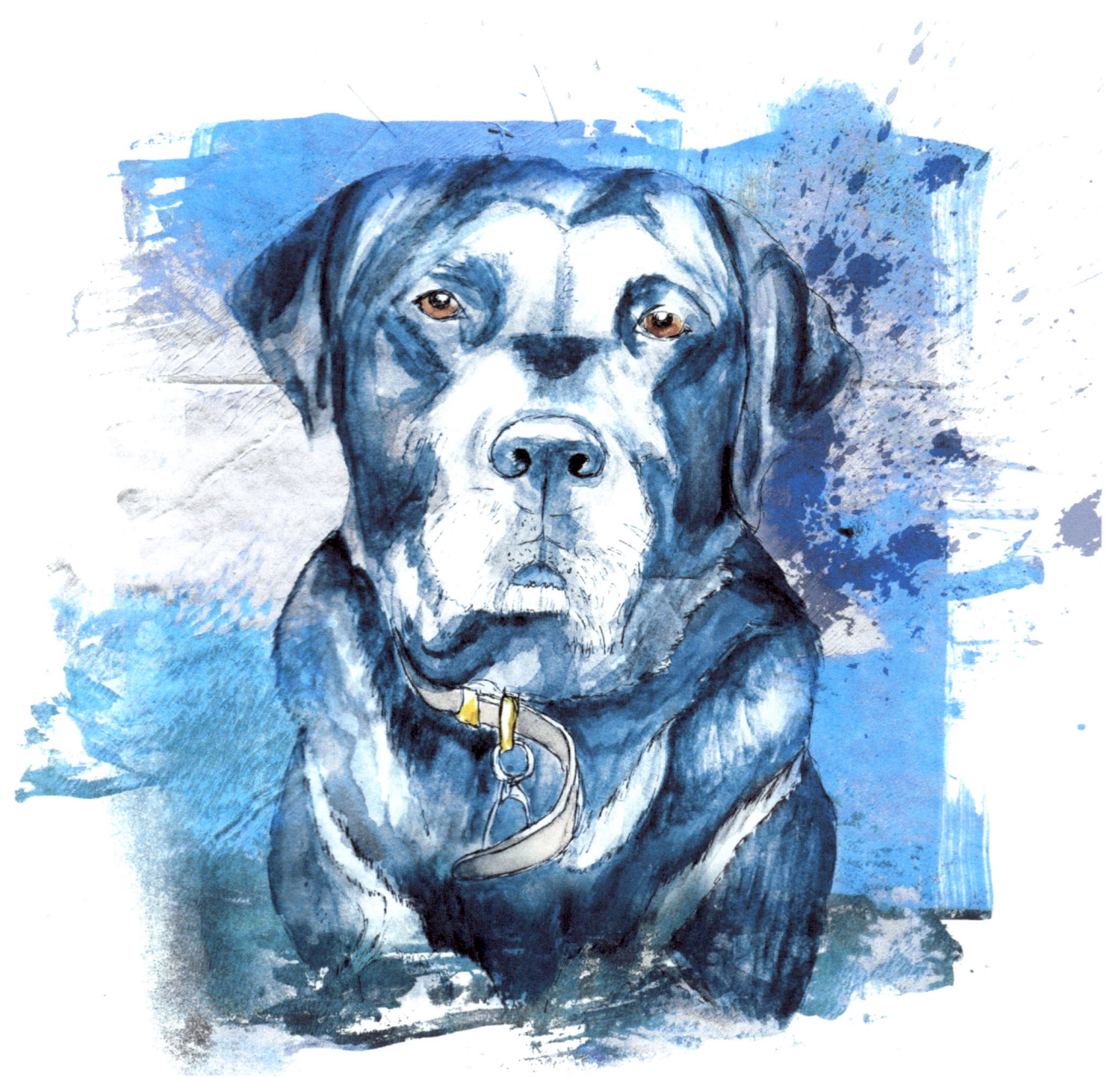

Milo: Nigel and Beckie Harris

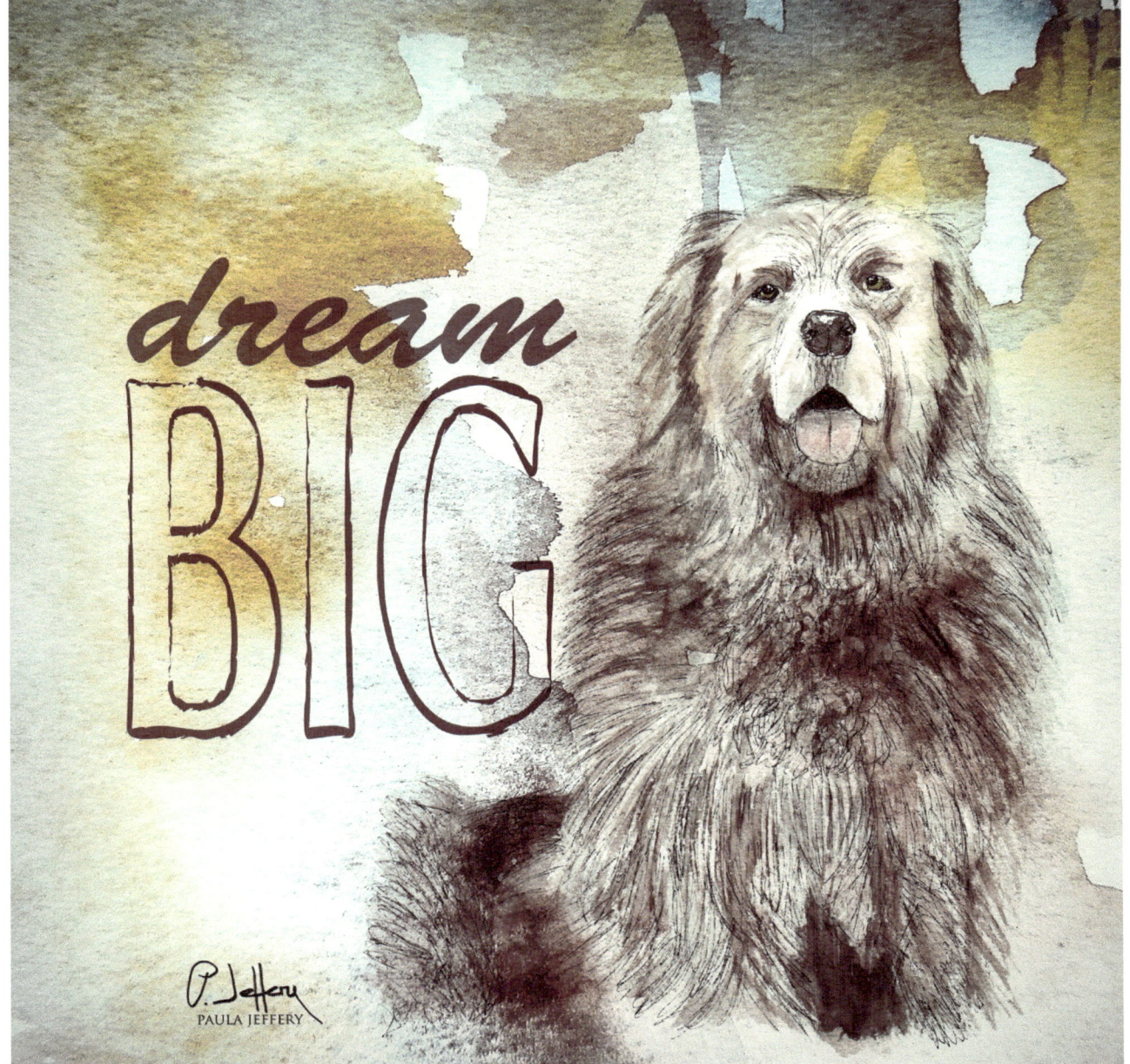

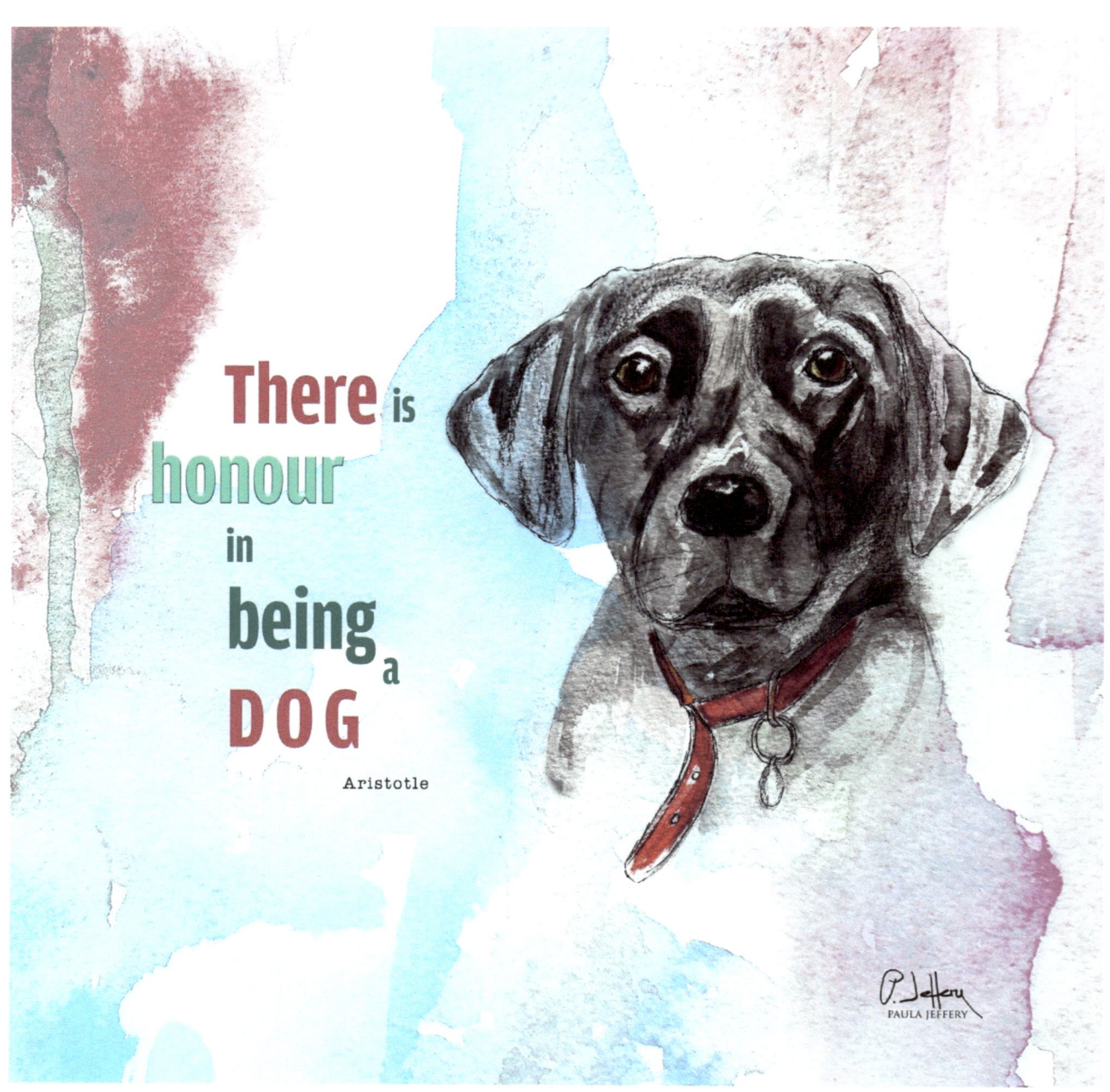

There is honour in being a DOG

Aristotle

Judy: Pete and Esther Jones

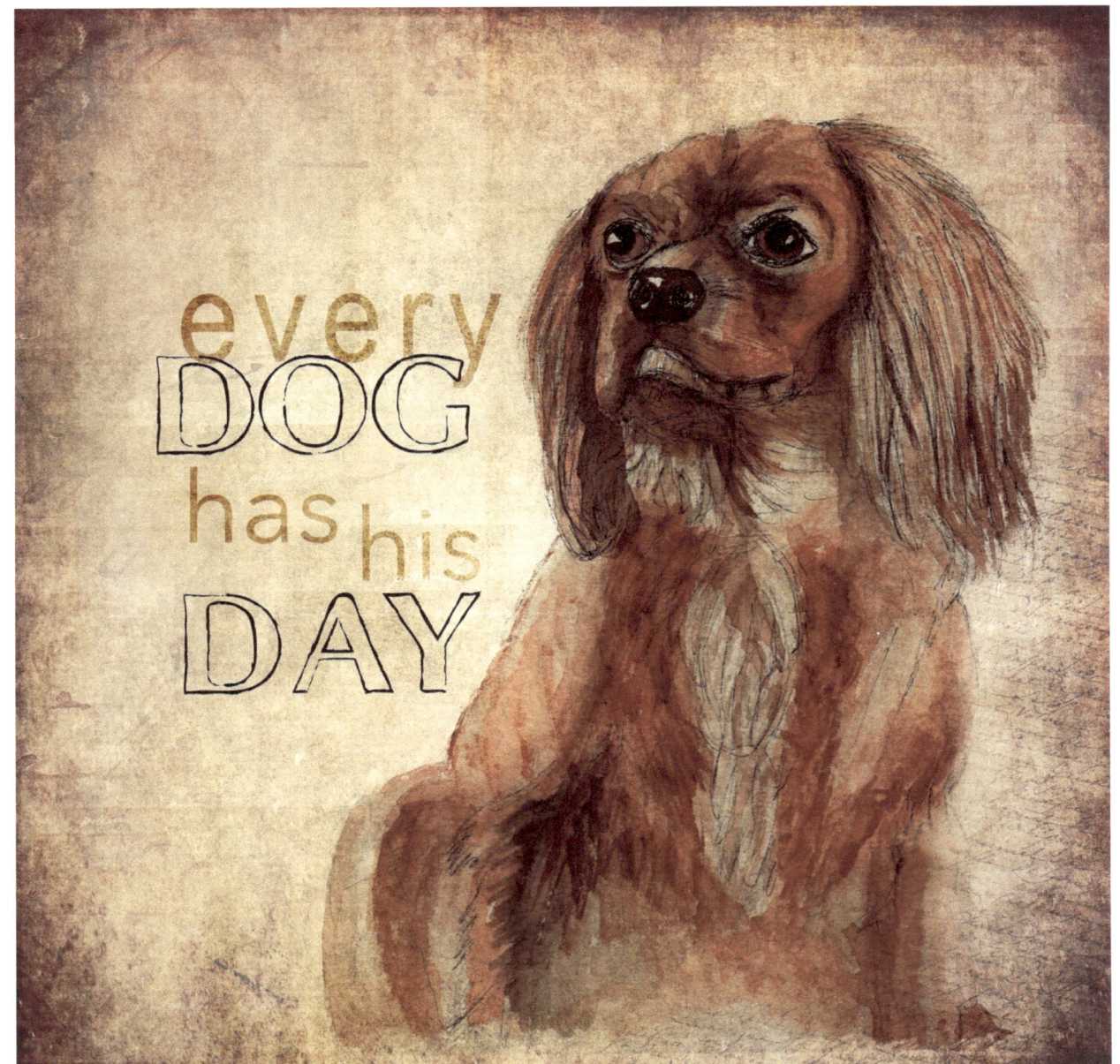

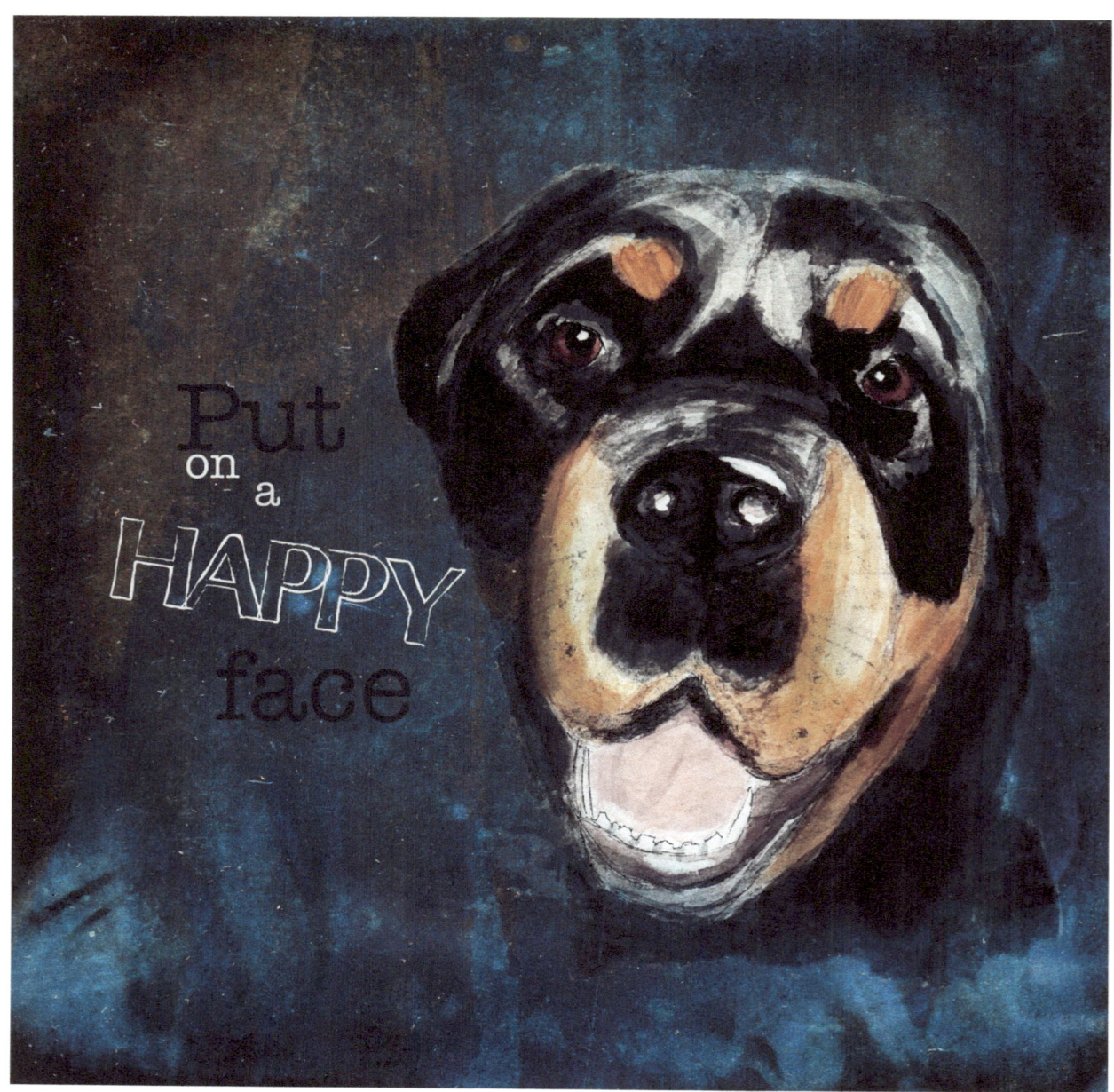

Bella: Ben Sanders and Kerry Burns

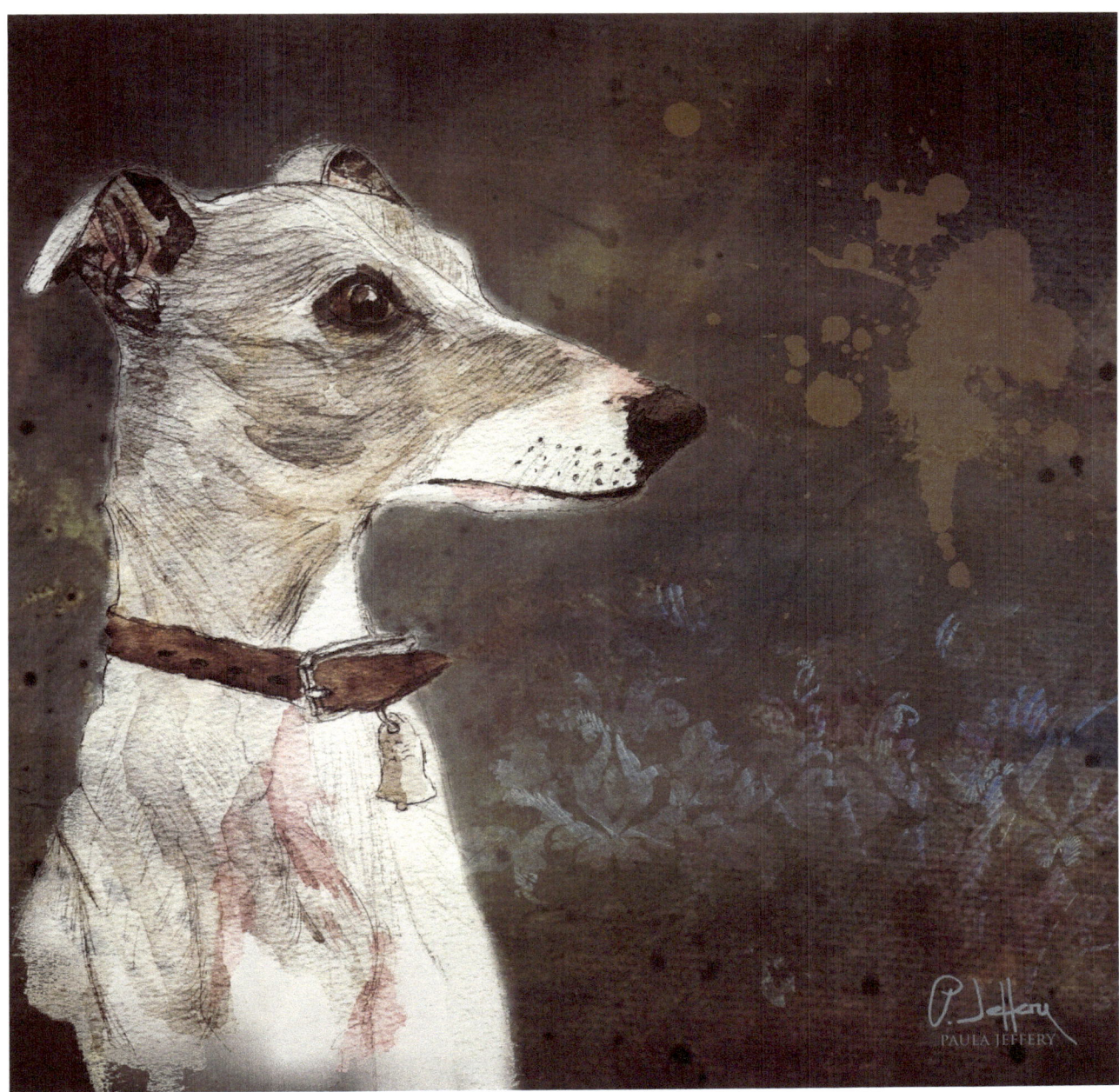

Harry: Nigel and Beckie Harris

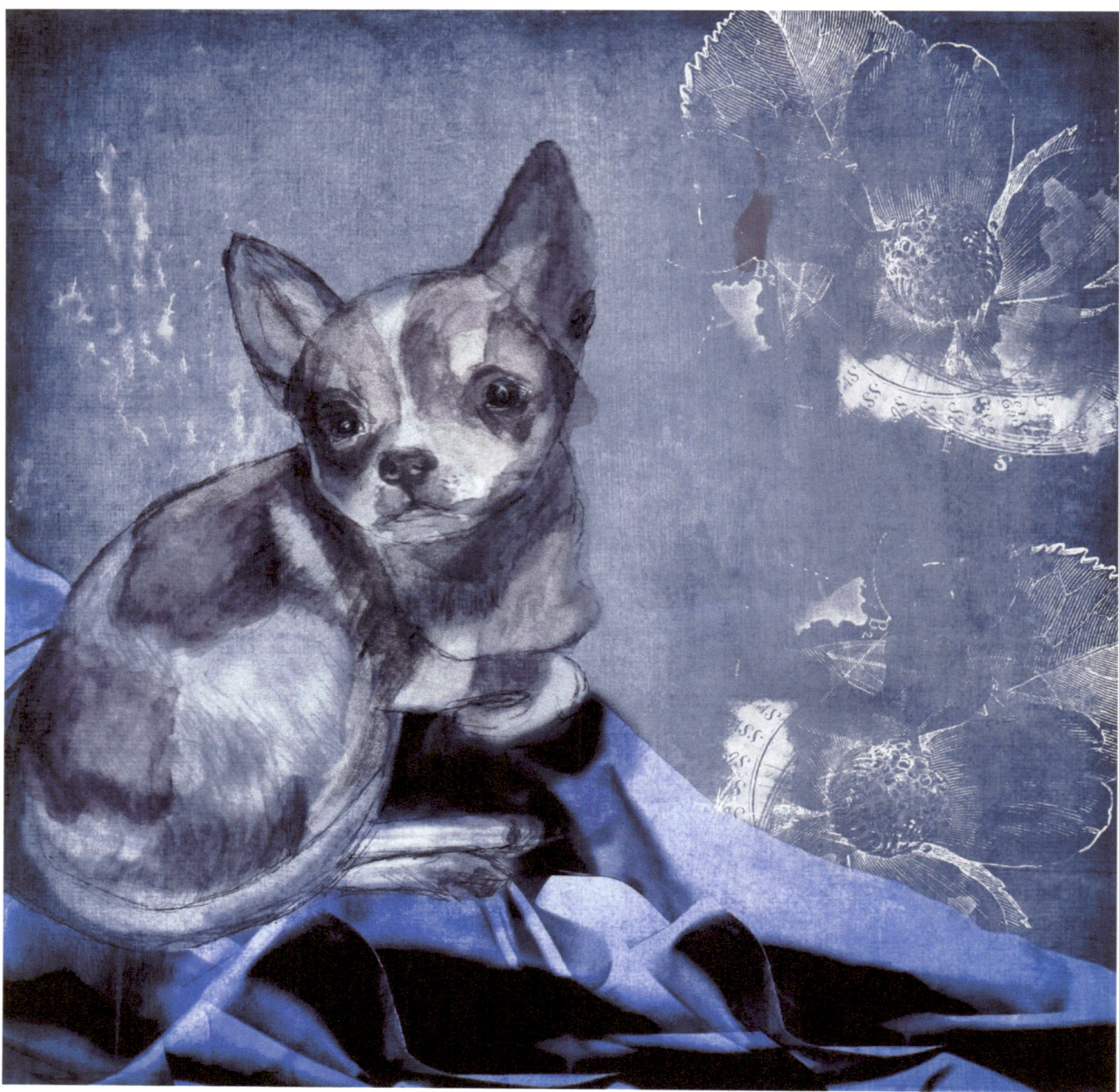

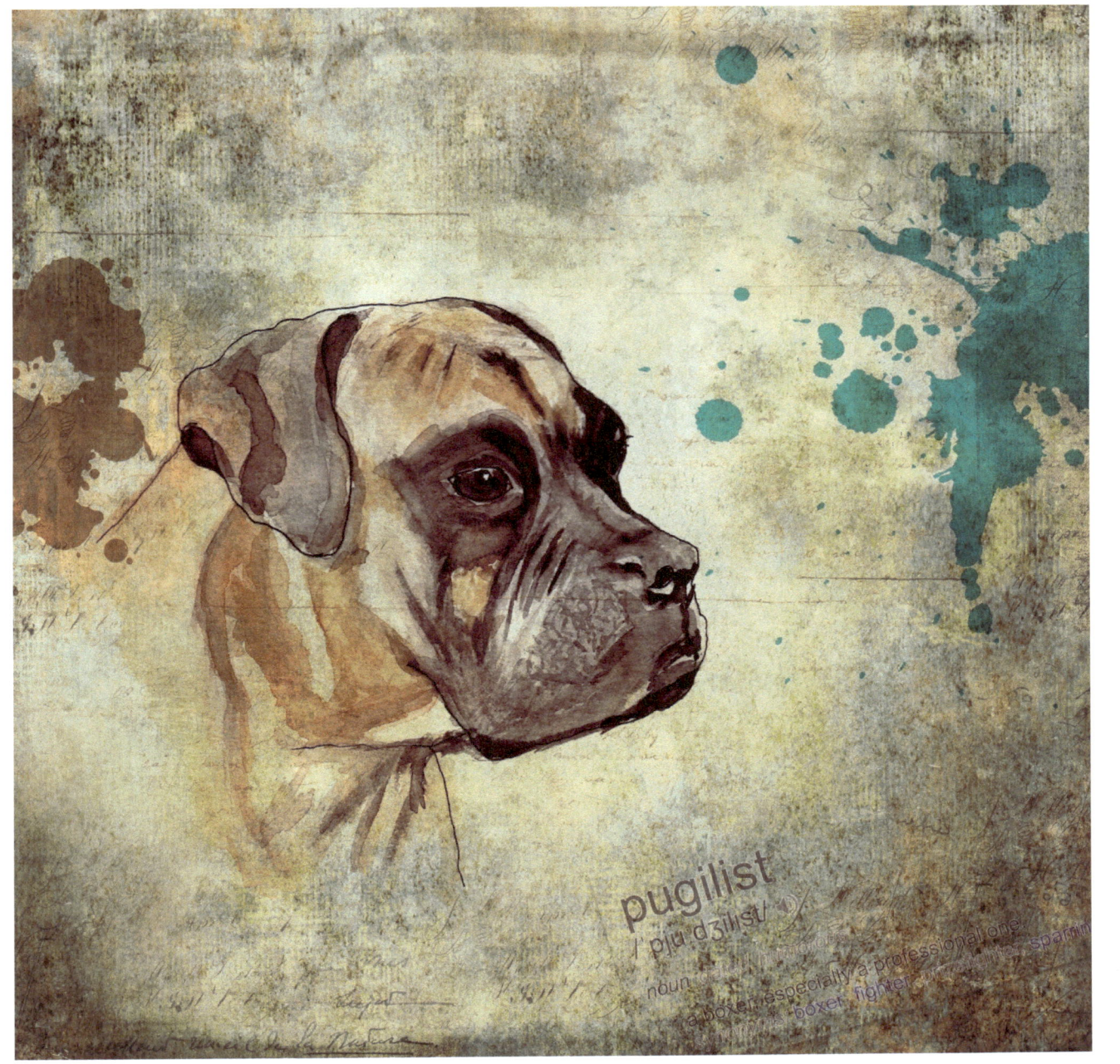

pugilist
| pjuːdʒɪlɪst |
noun
a boxer, especially a professional one.
boxer, fighter, ... sparring

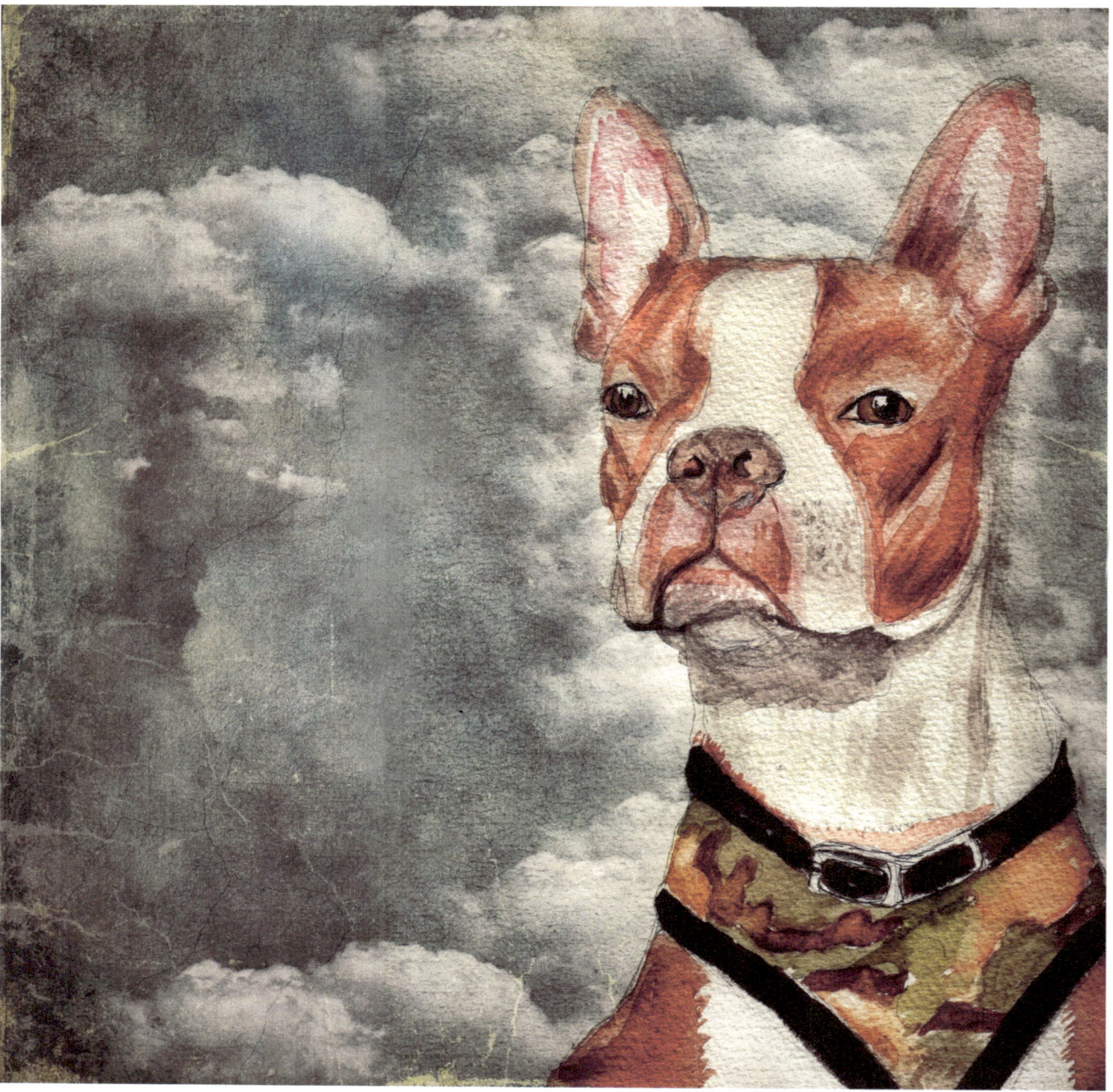

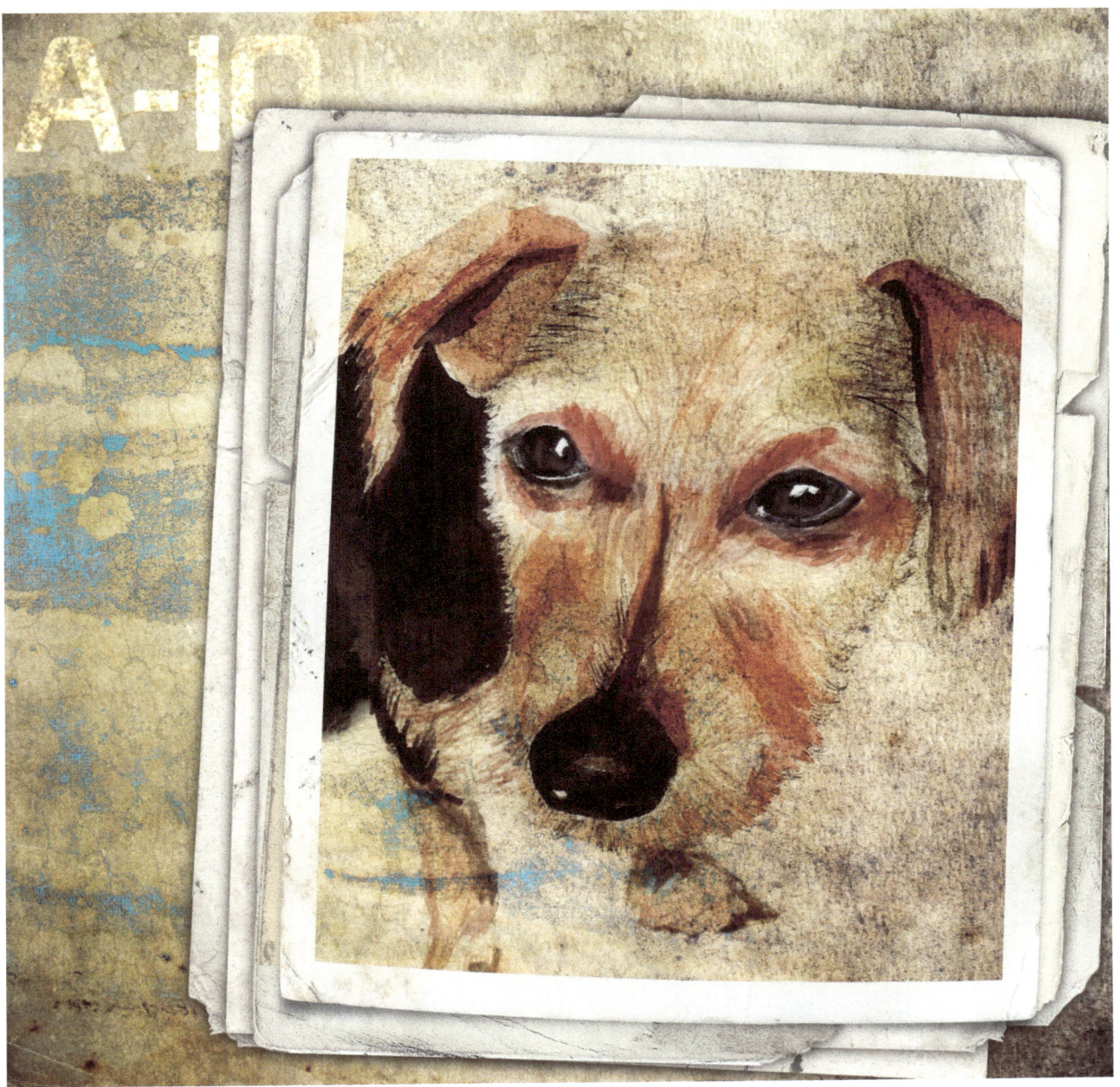

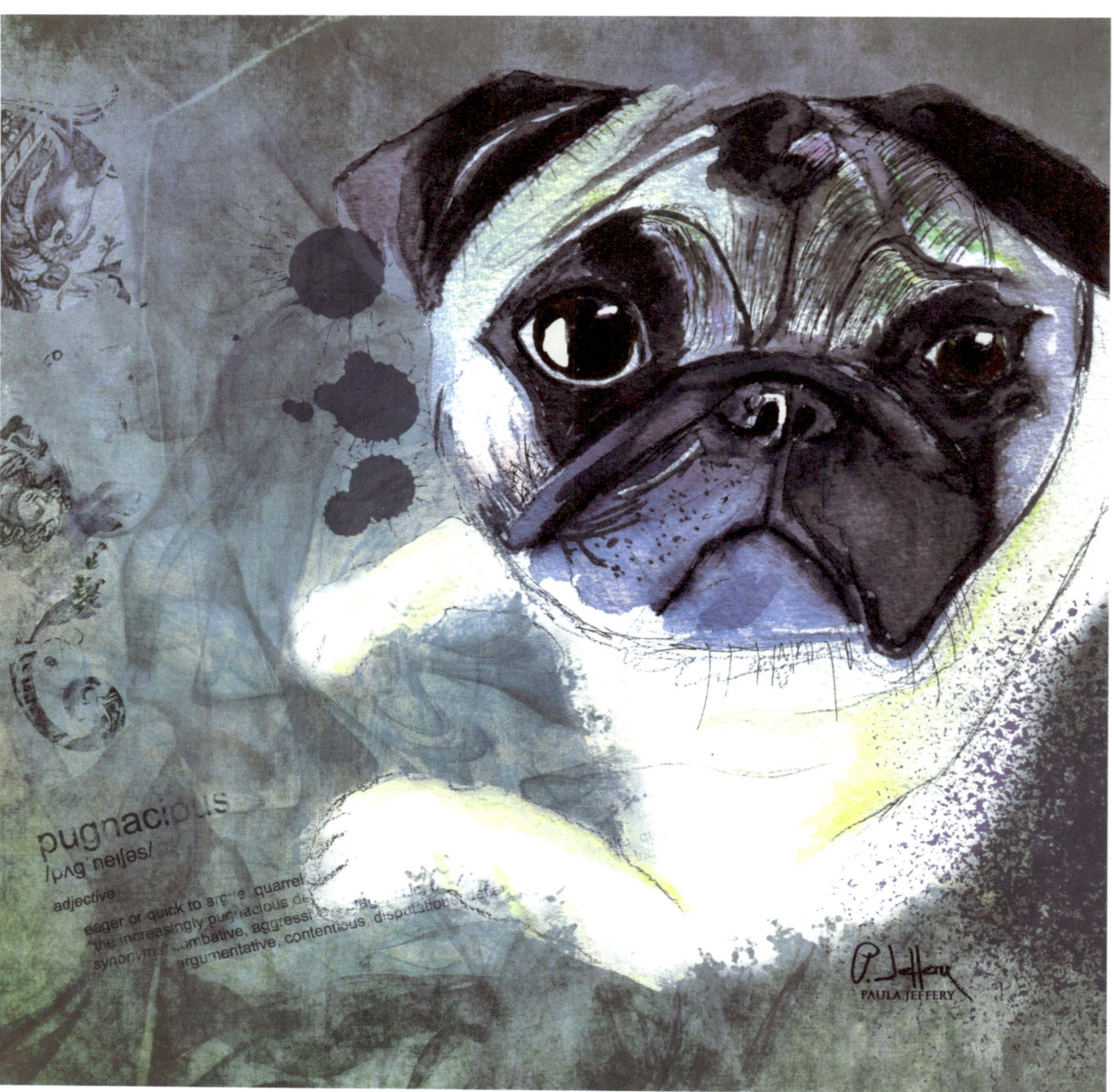

pugnacious
/pʌɡ neɪʃəs/

adjective

eager or quick to argue, quarrel [...]
"the increasingly pugnacious de[...]"
synonyms: combative, aggressi[...] [...]
argumentative, contentious, disputatious [...]

PAULA JEFFERY

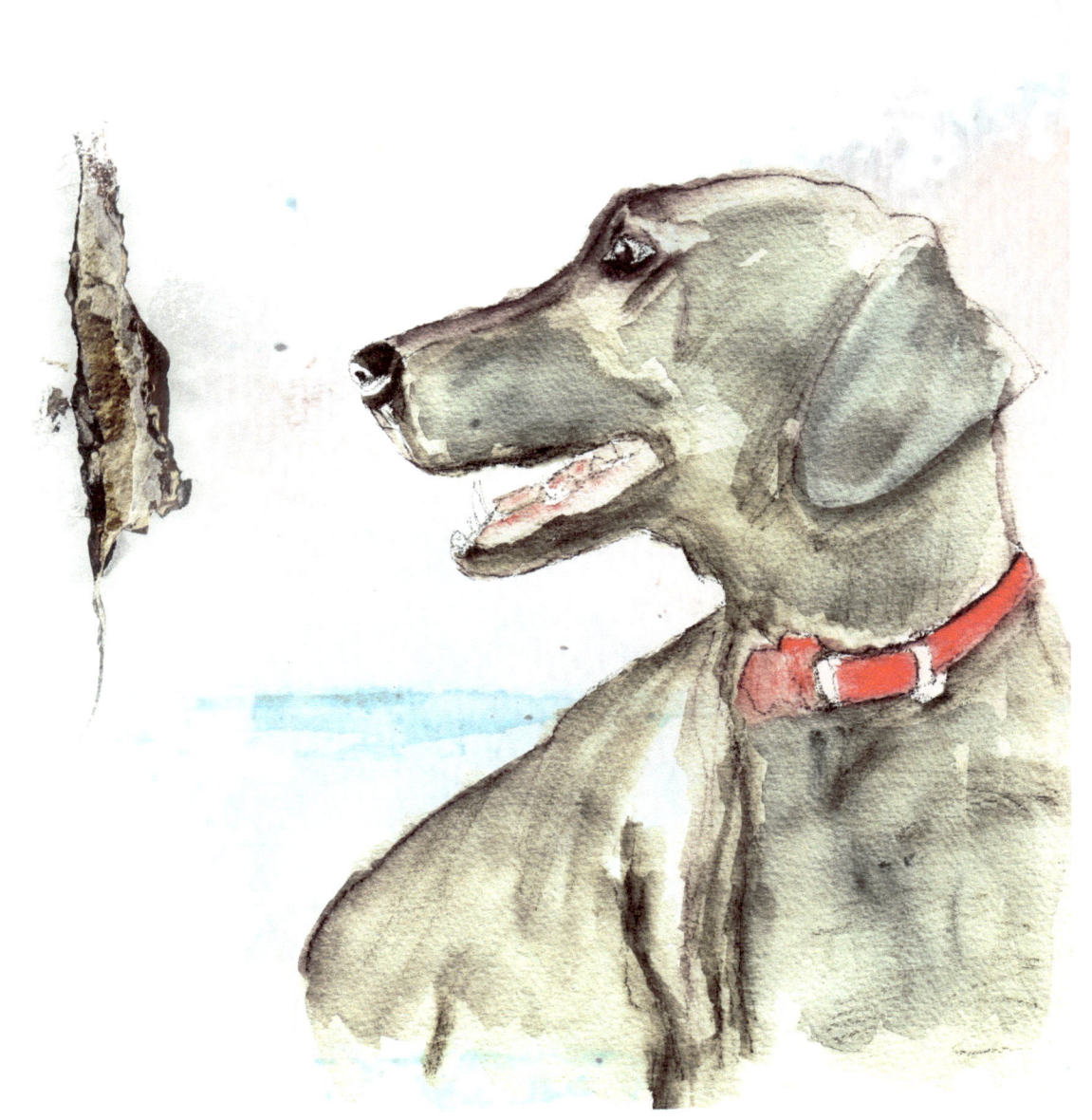

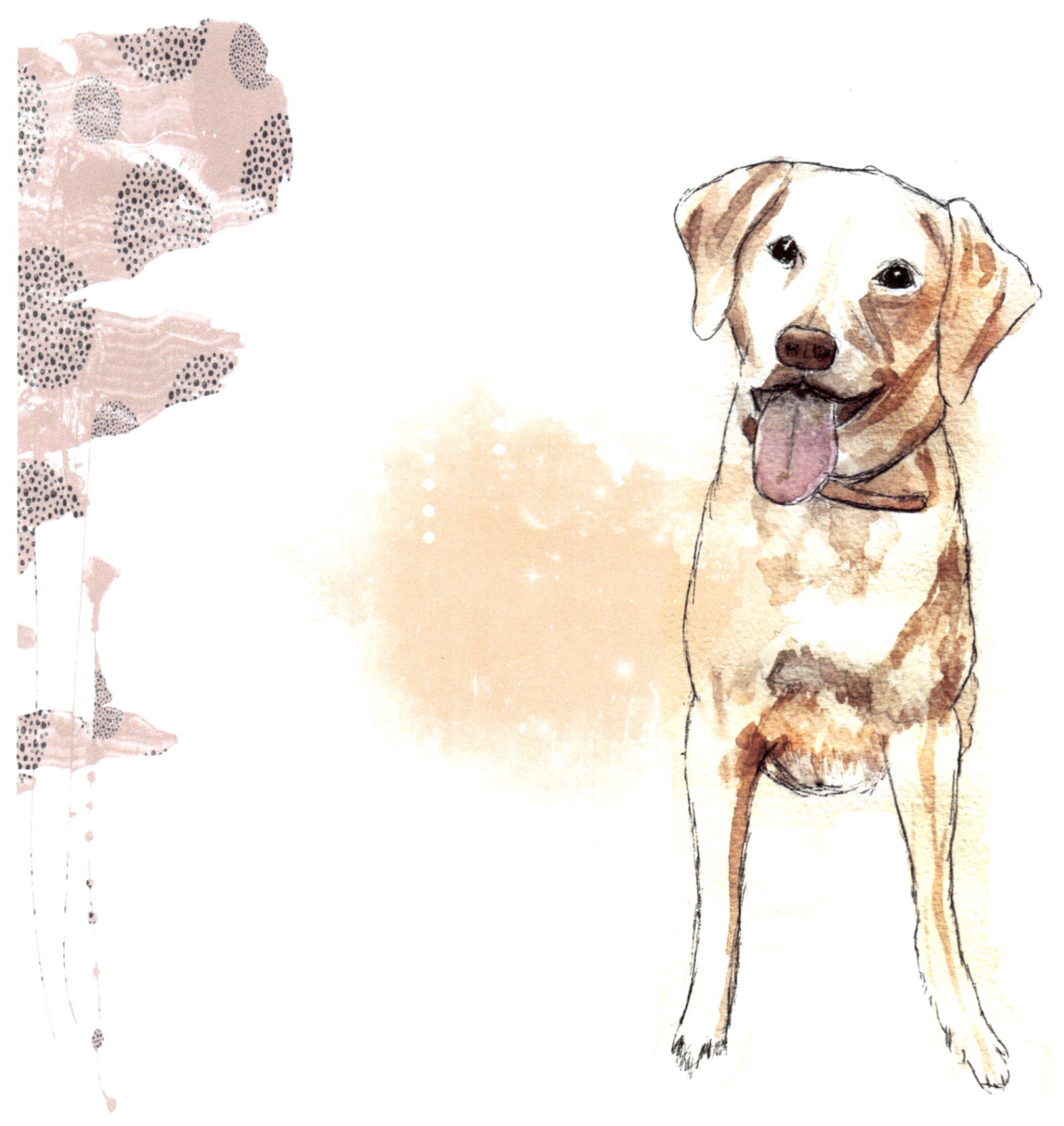

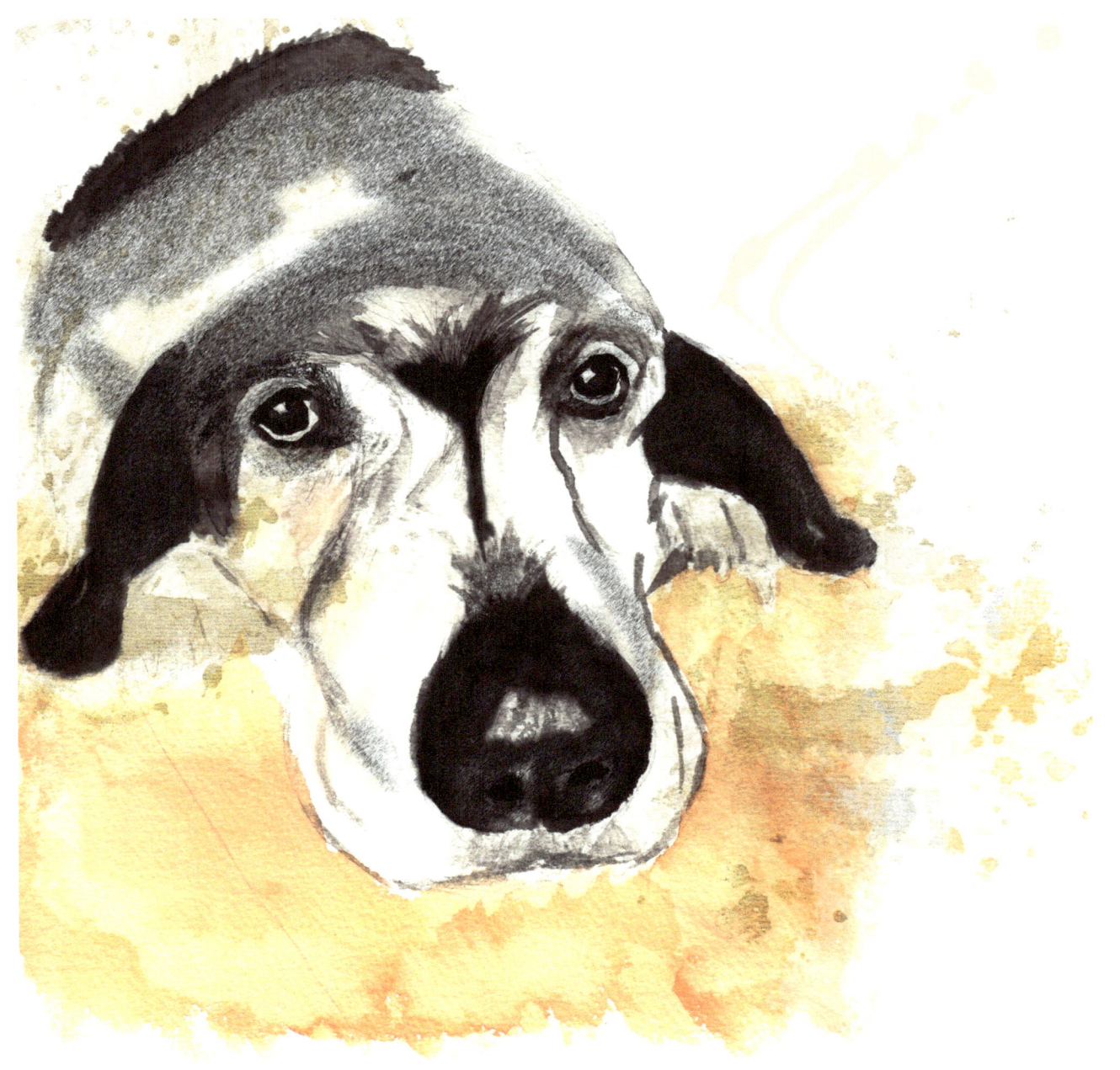

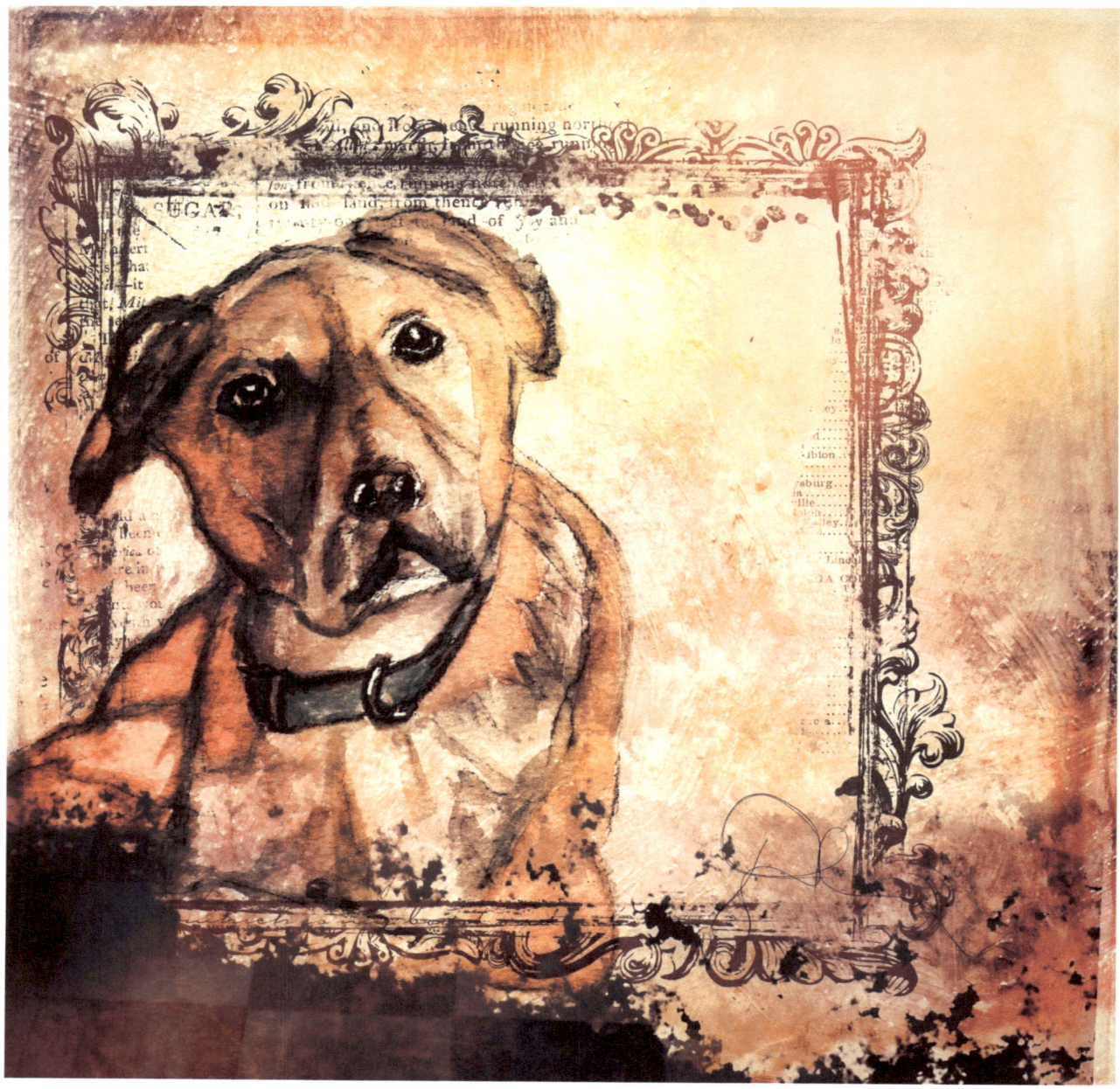

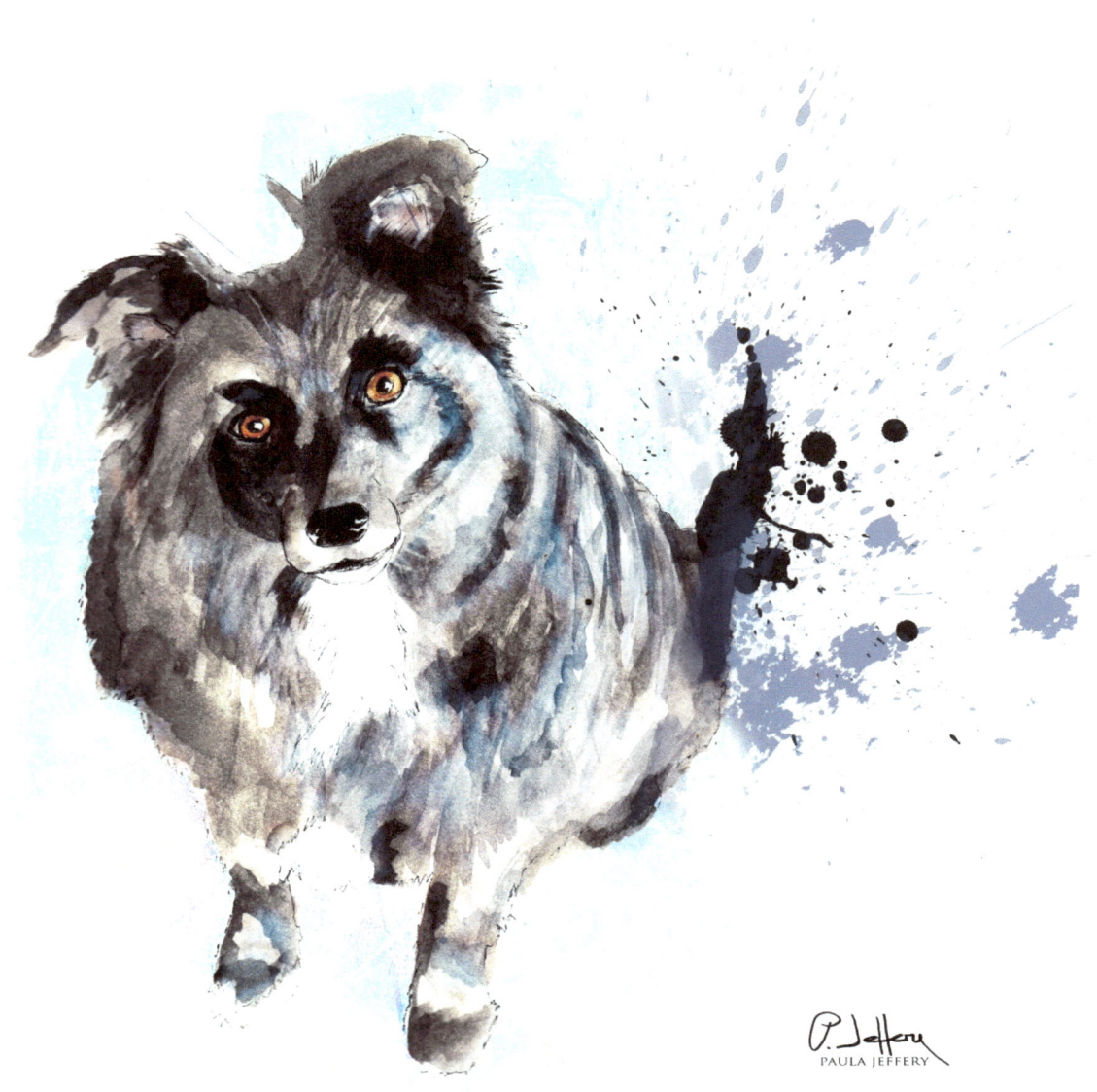

Pepper: Jane Mruk

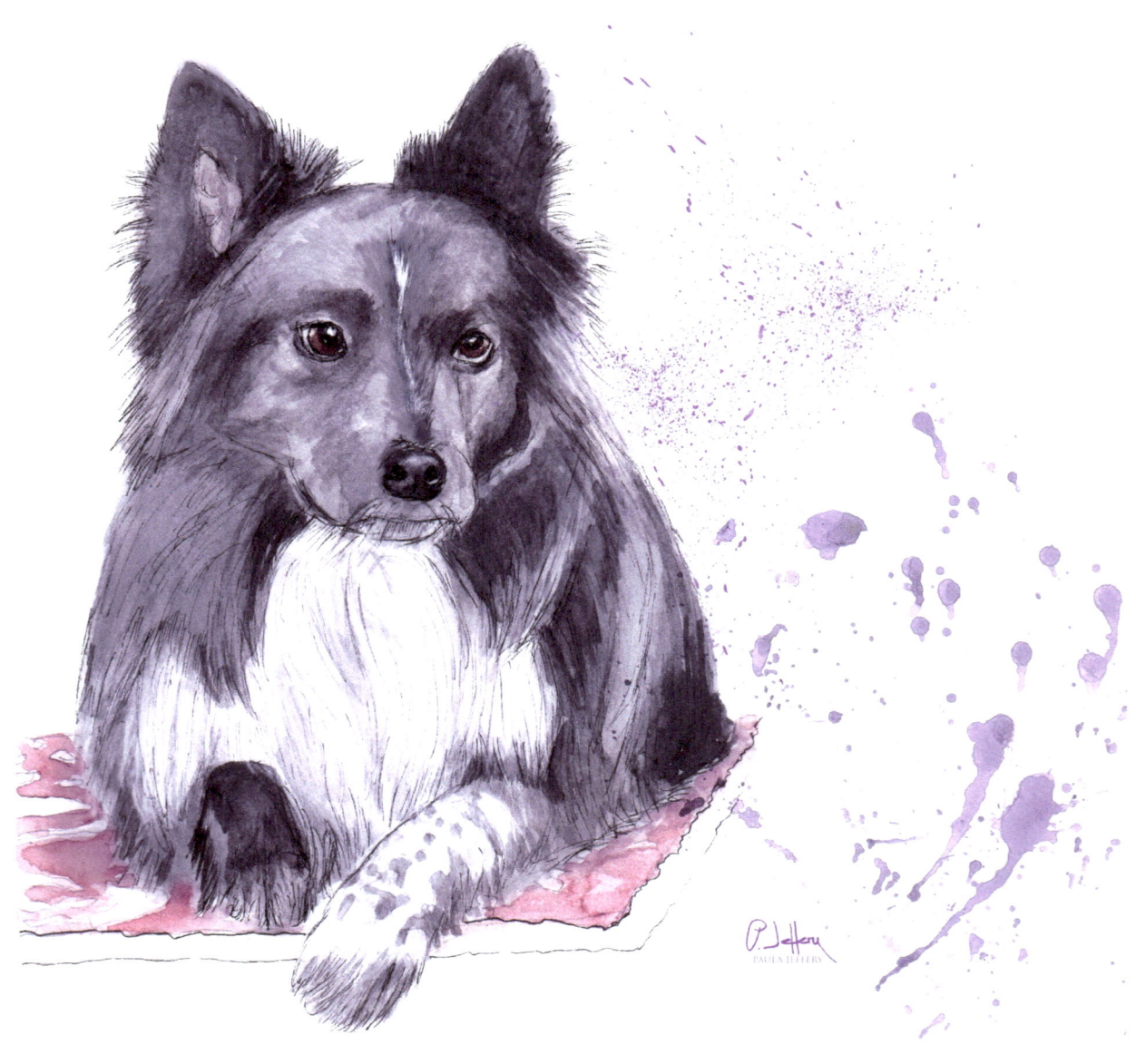

Porkchop: Jane Mruk

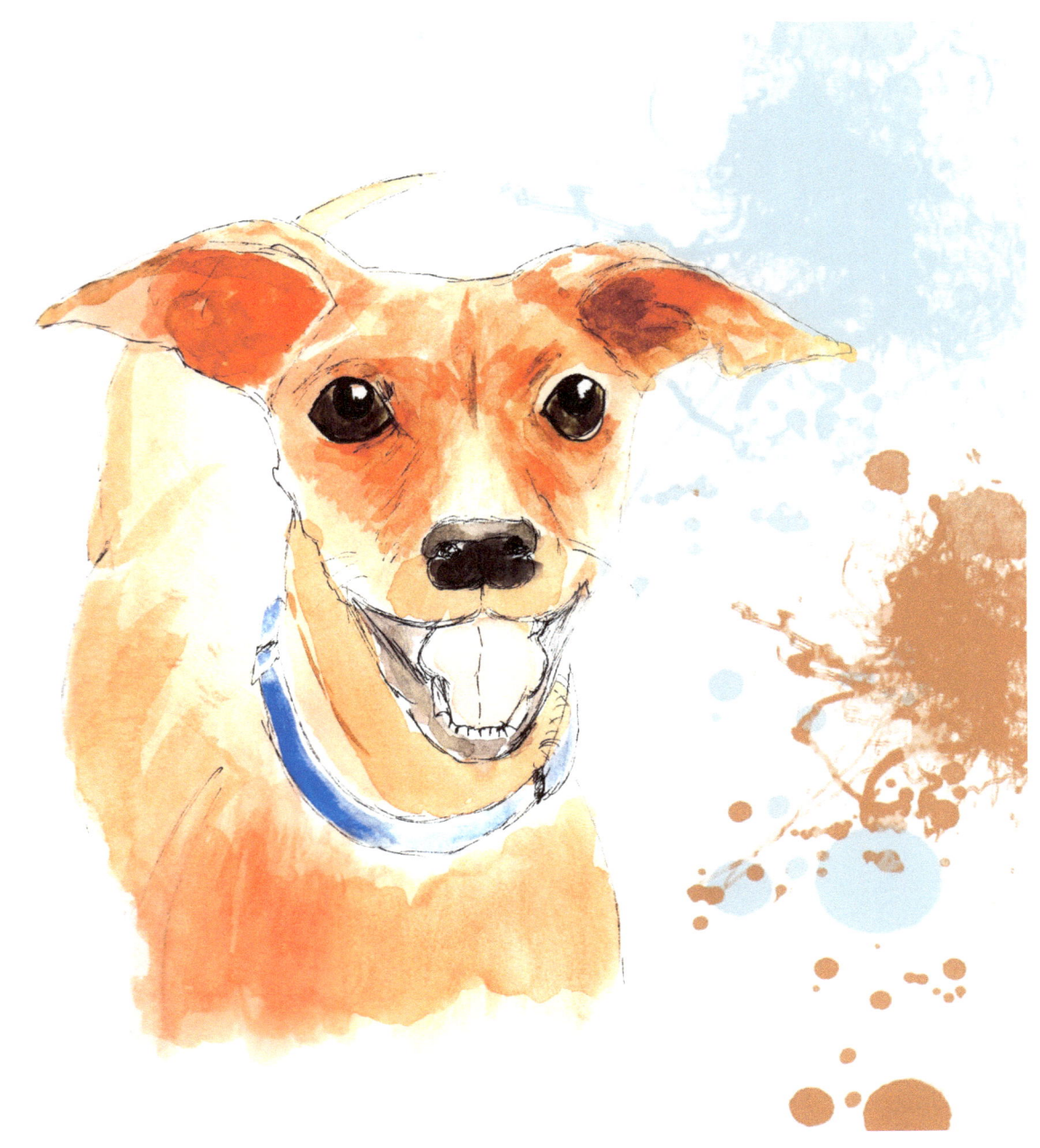

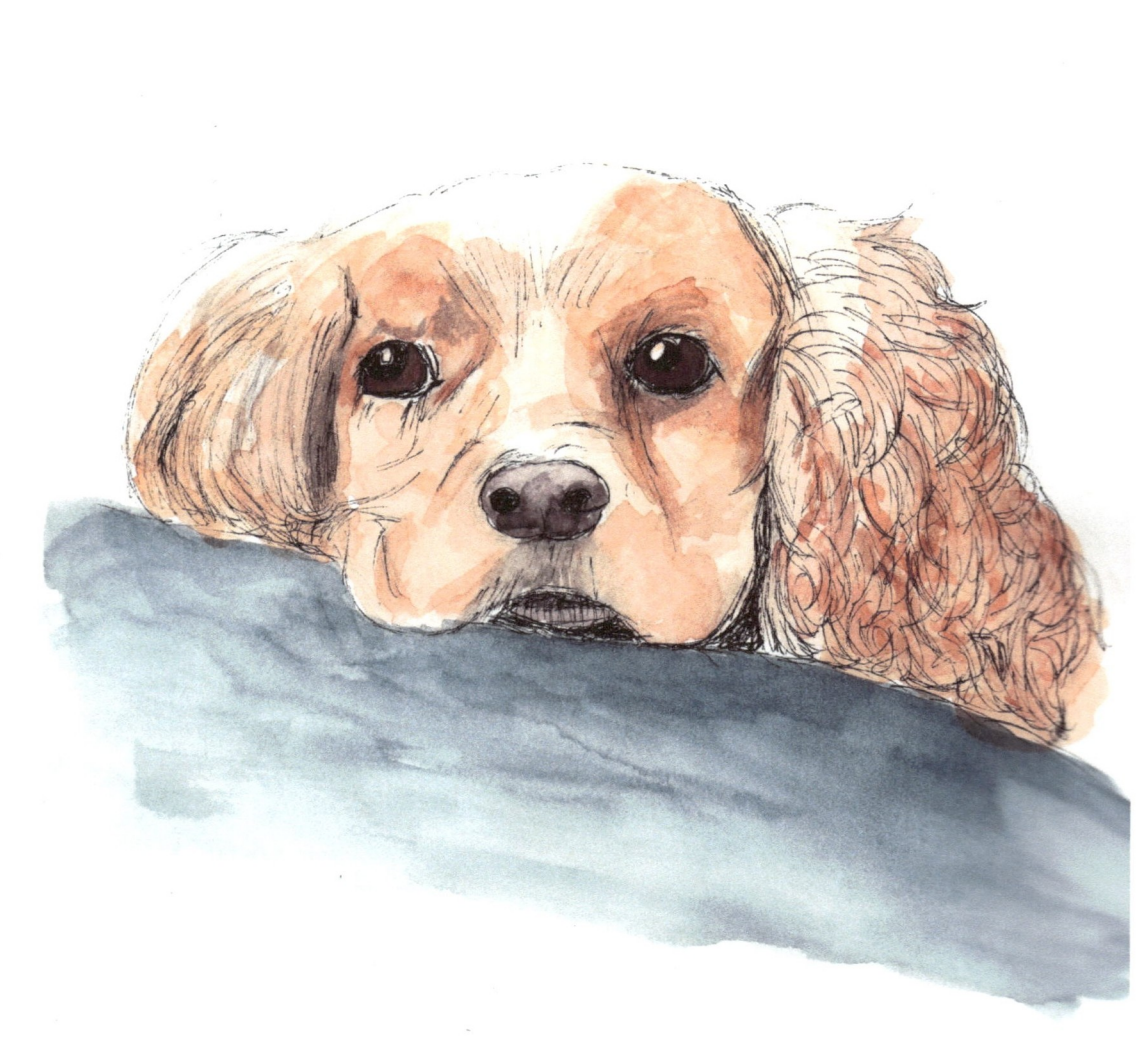

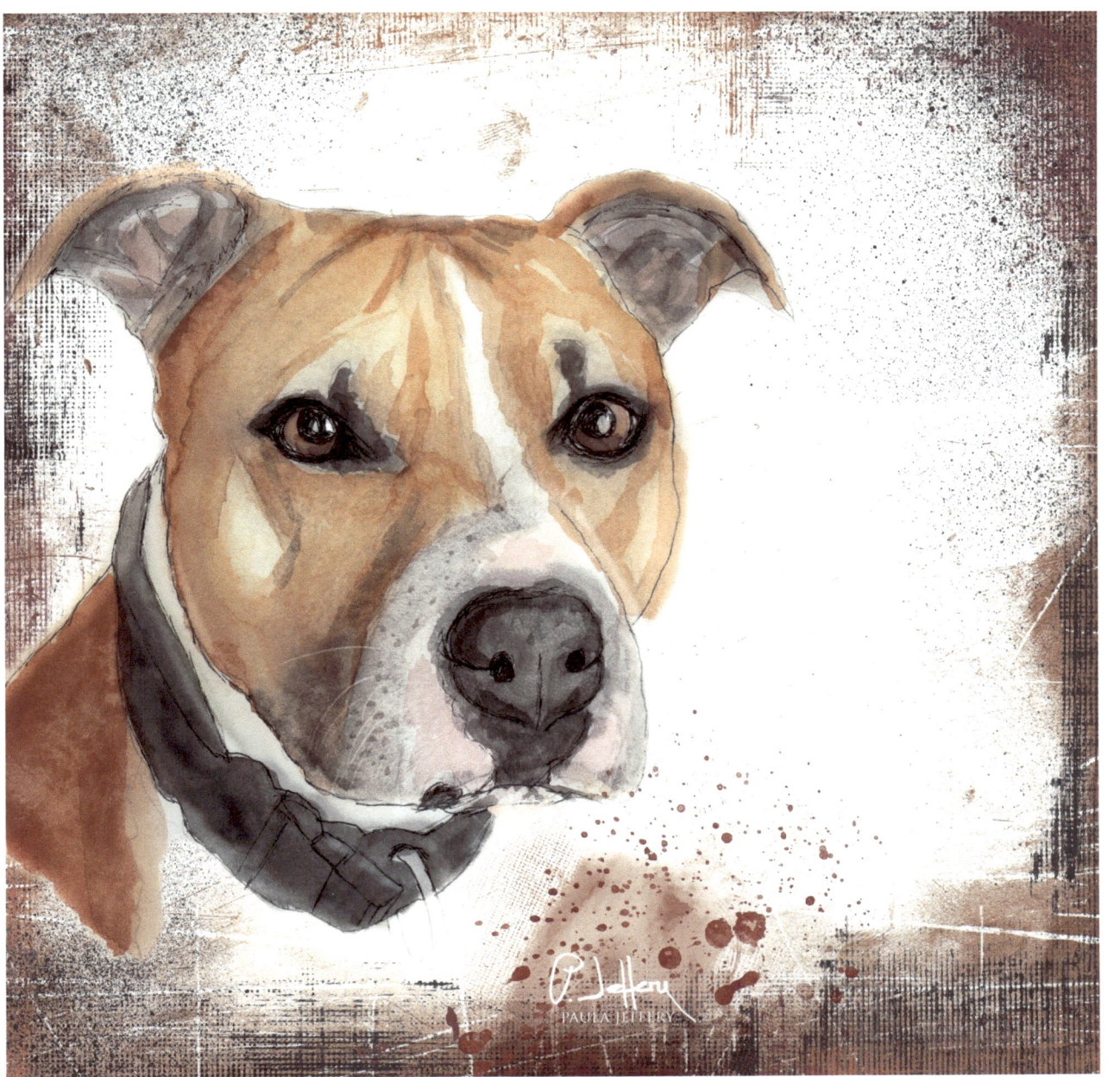

PAULA JEFFERY

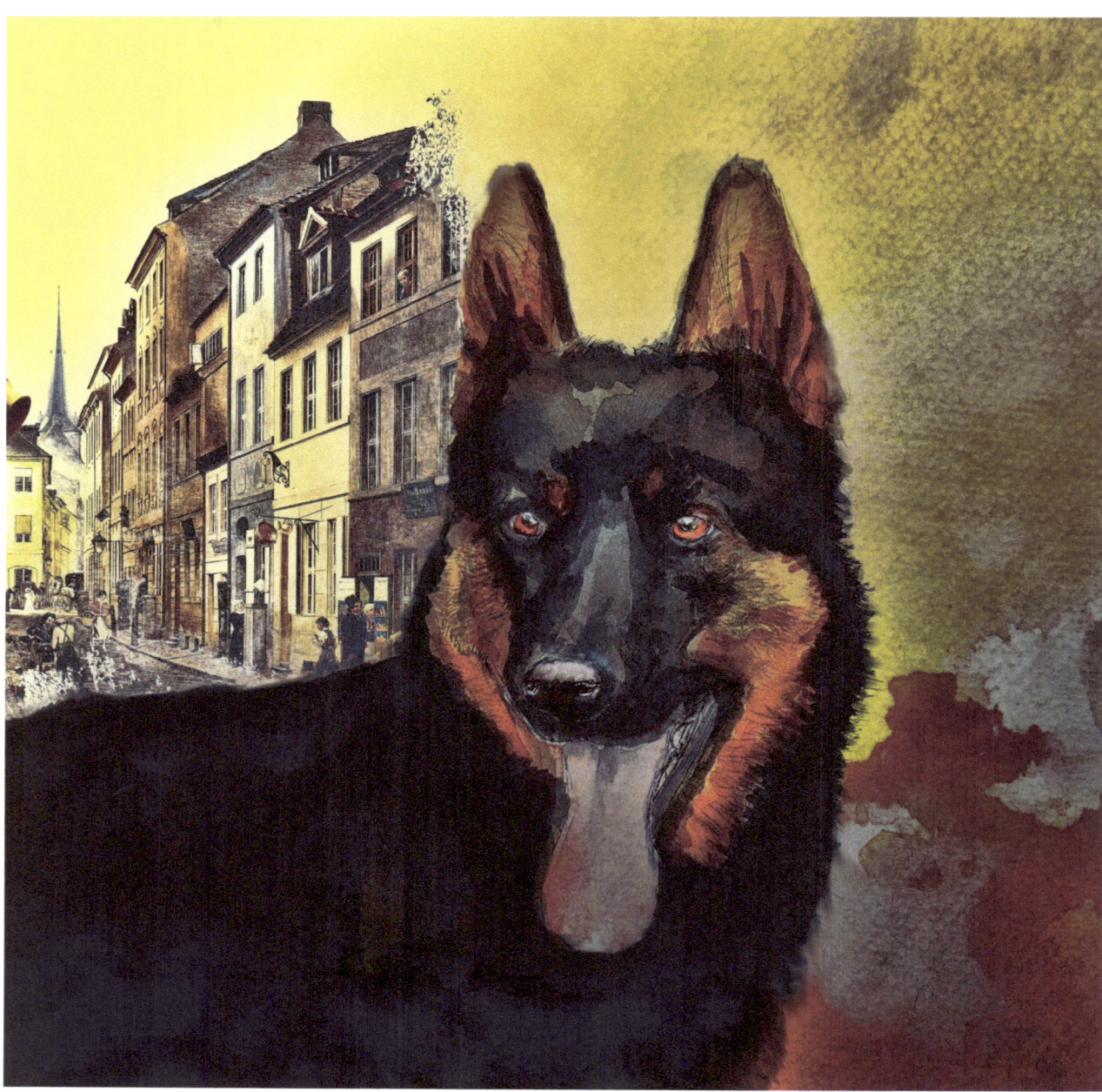

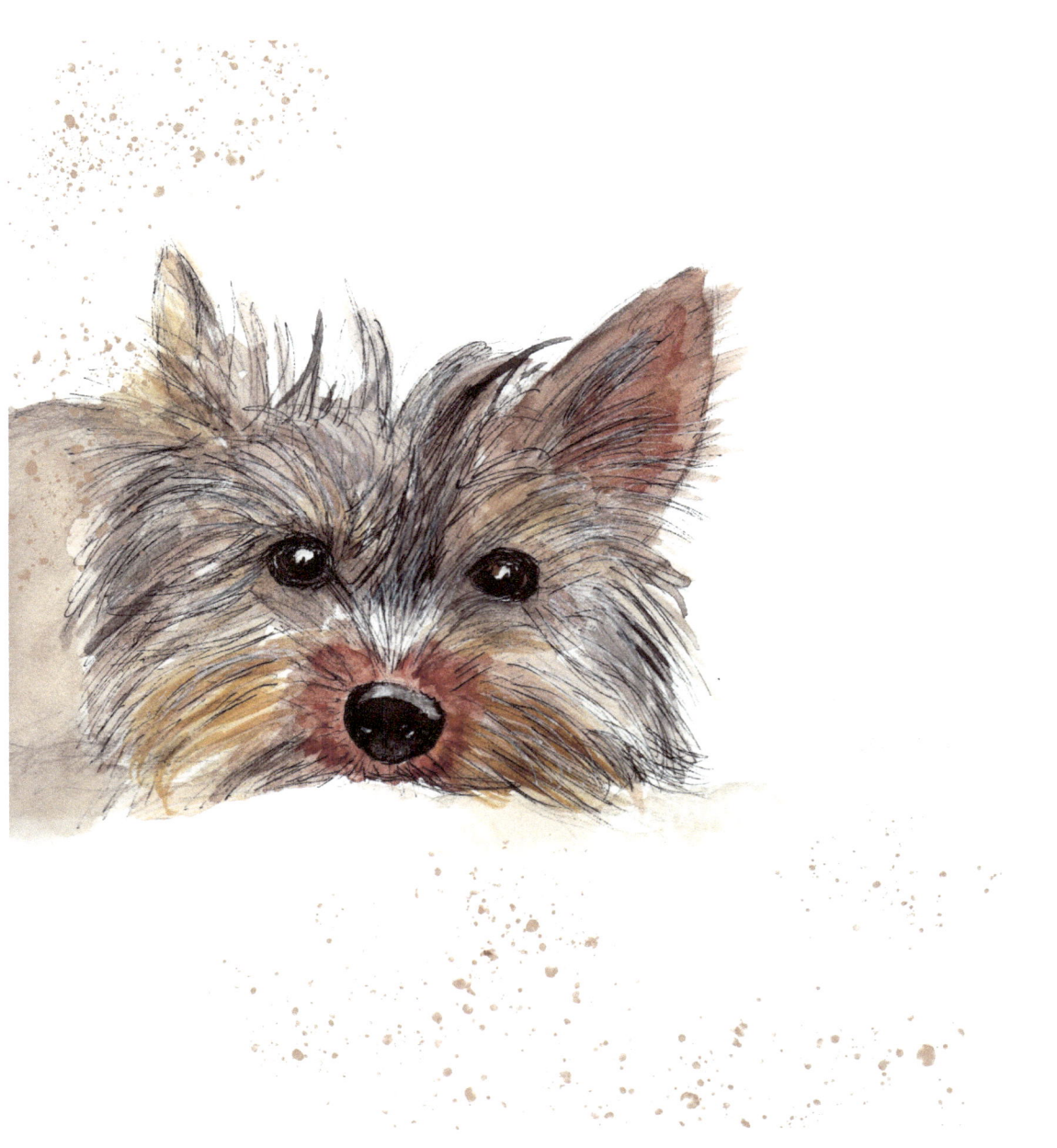

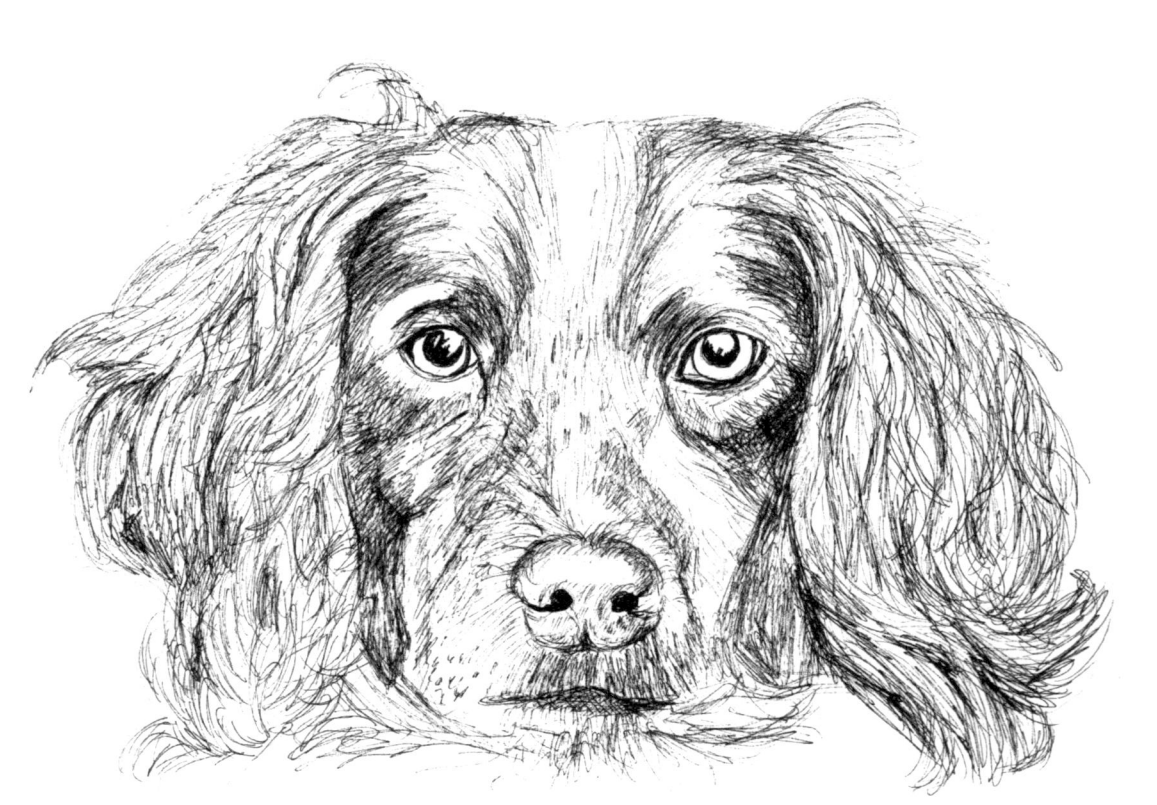

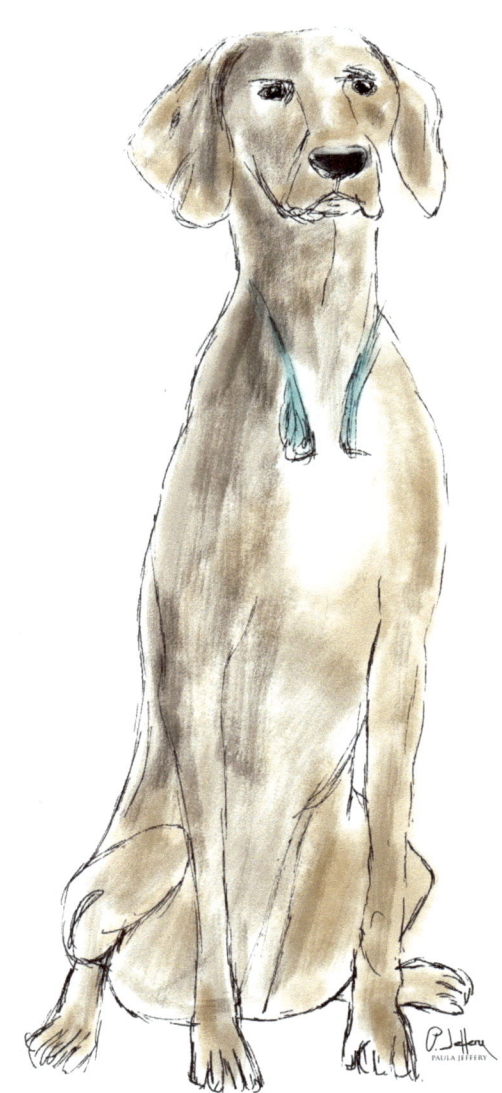

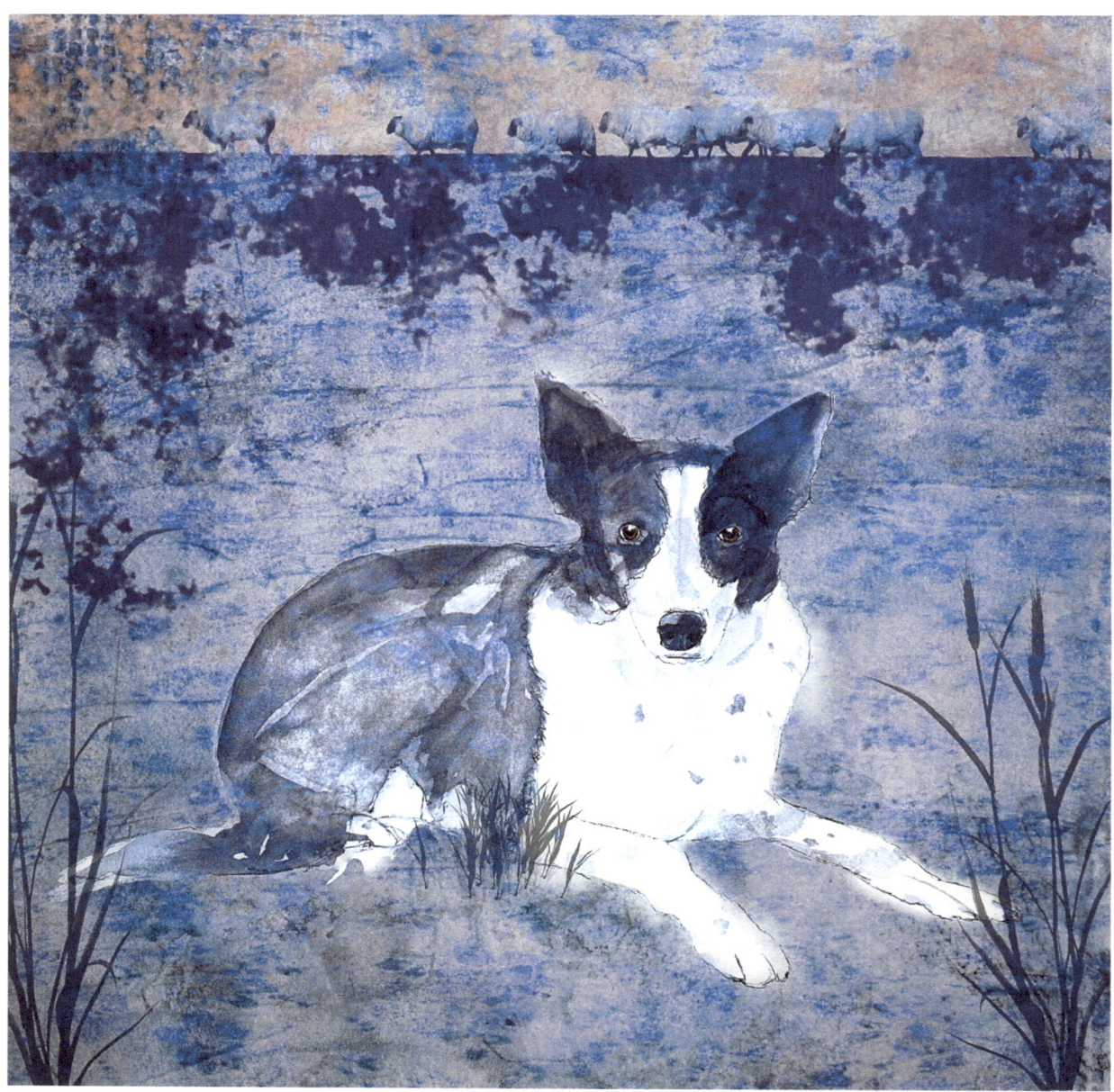

Milo: Beckie Allen and Jack Allen

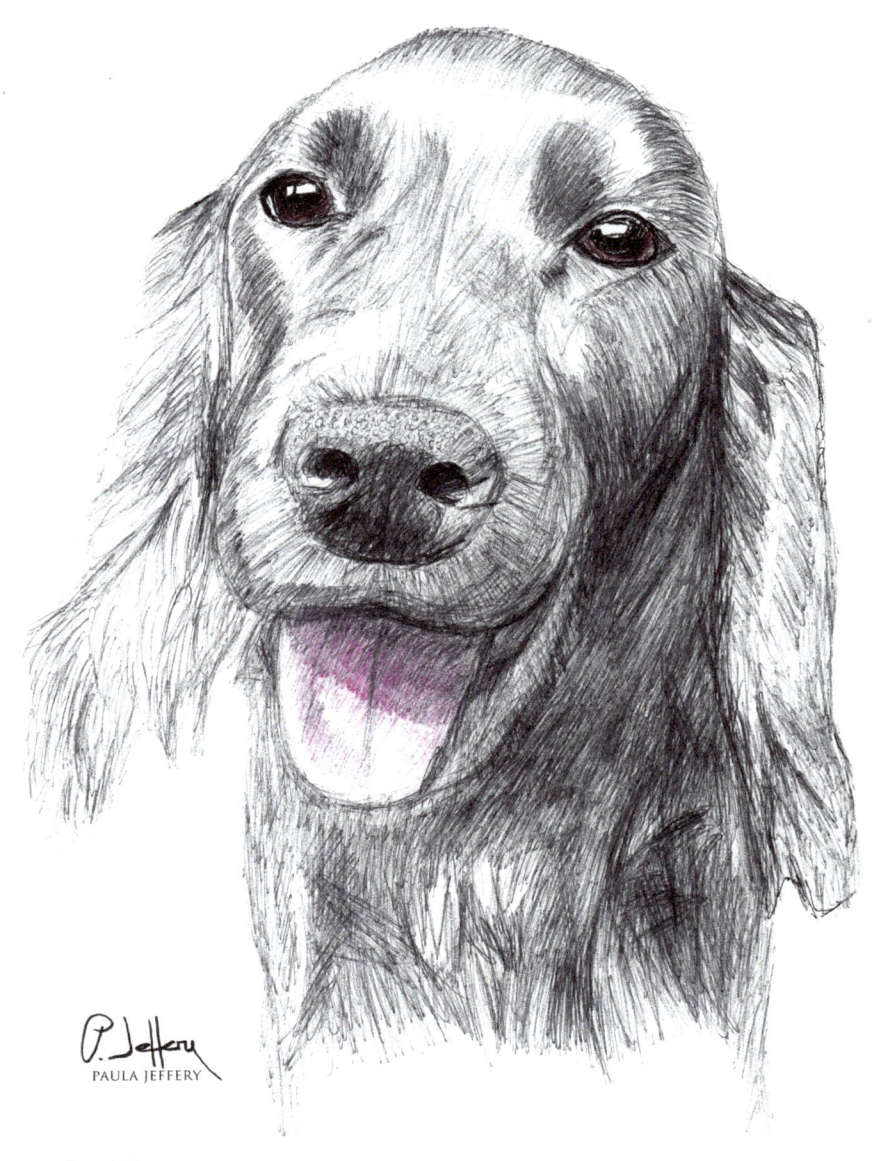

PAULA JEFFERY

Tess: Becky Allen

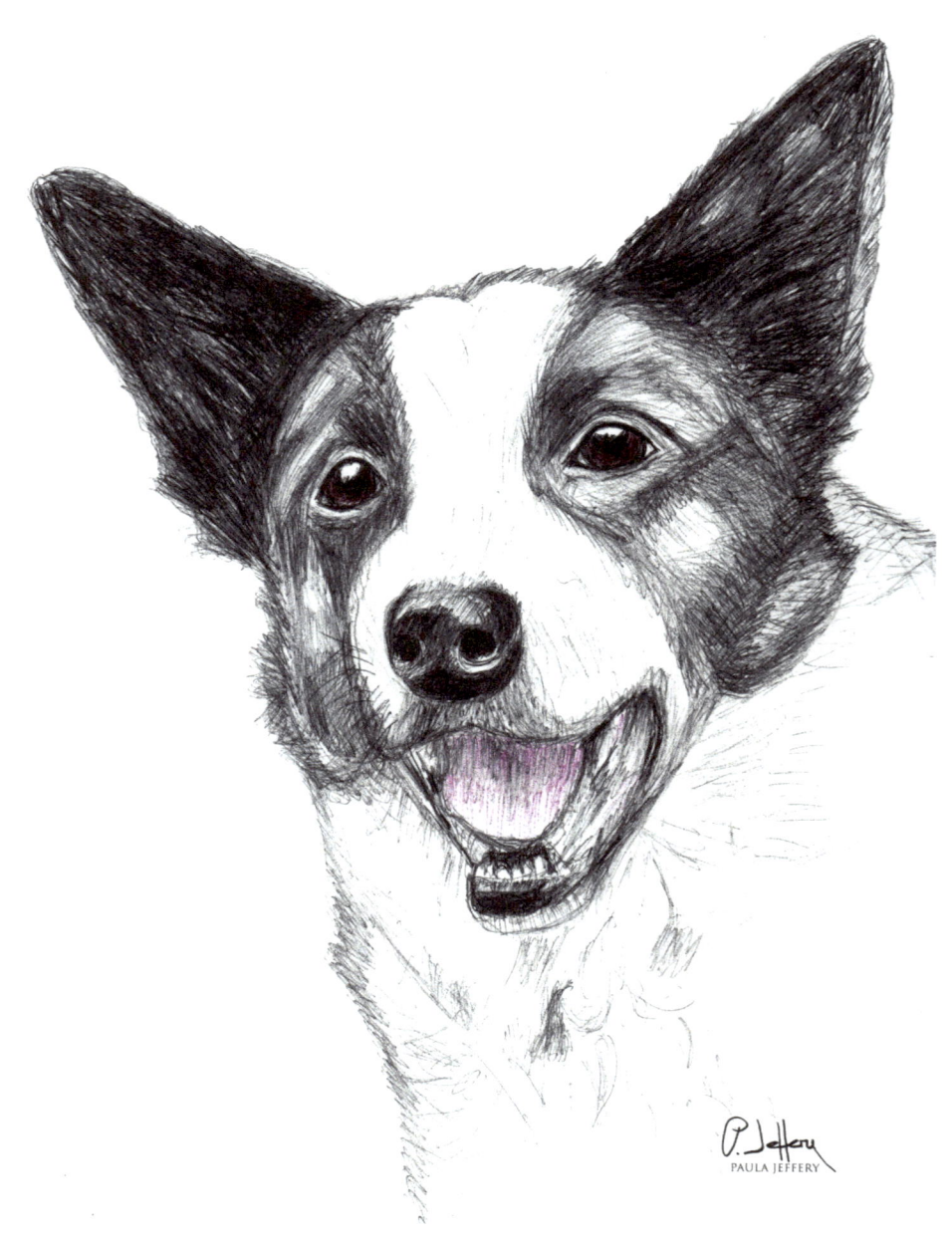

Milo: Becky Allen and Jack Allen

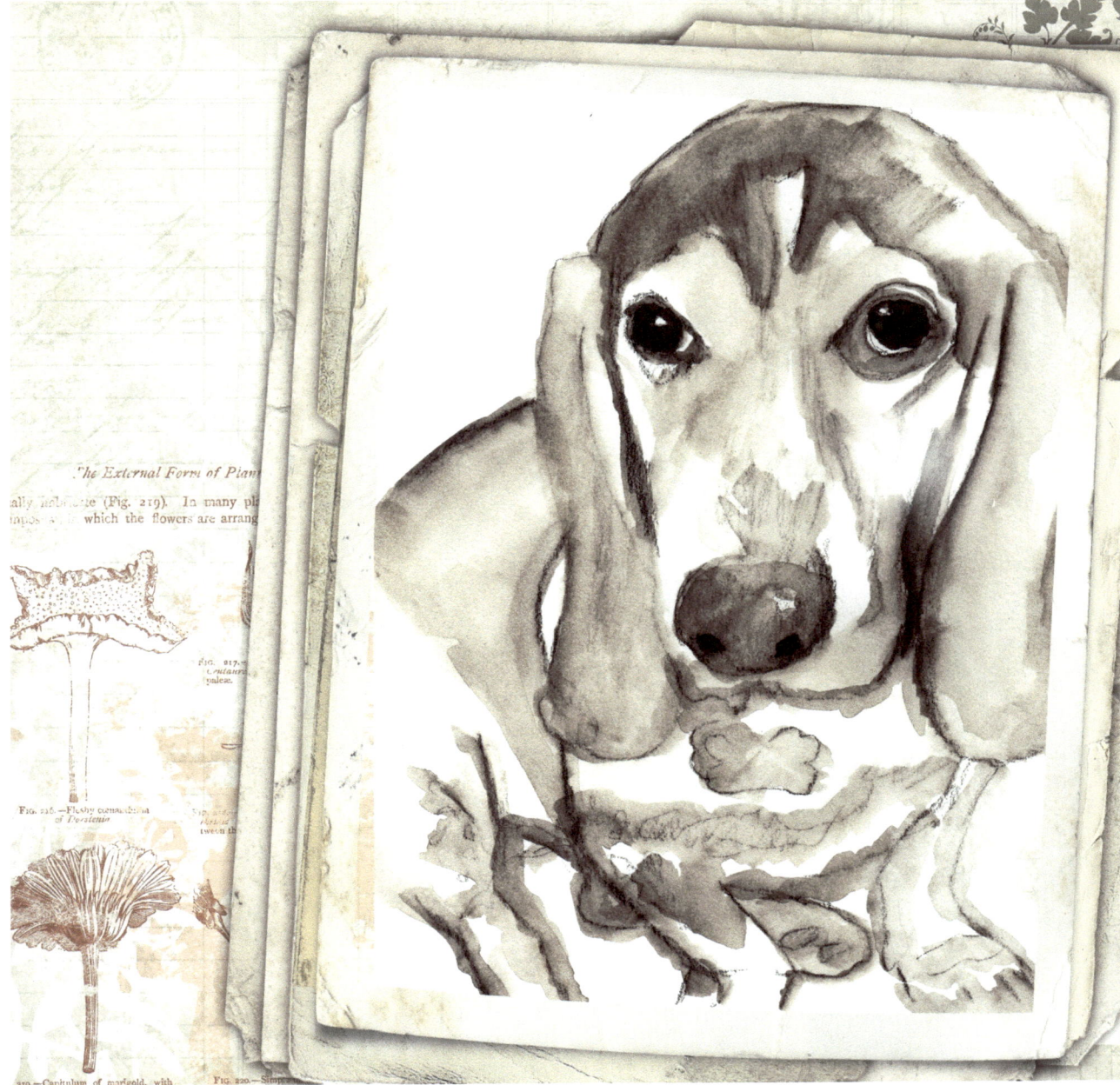

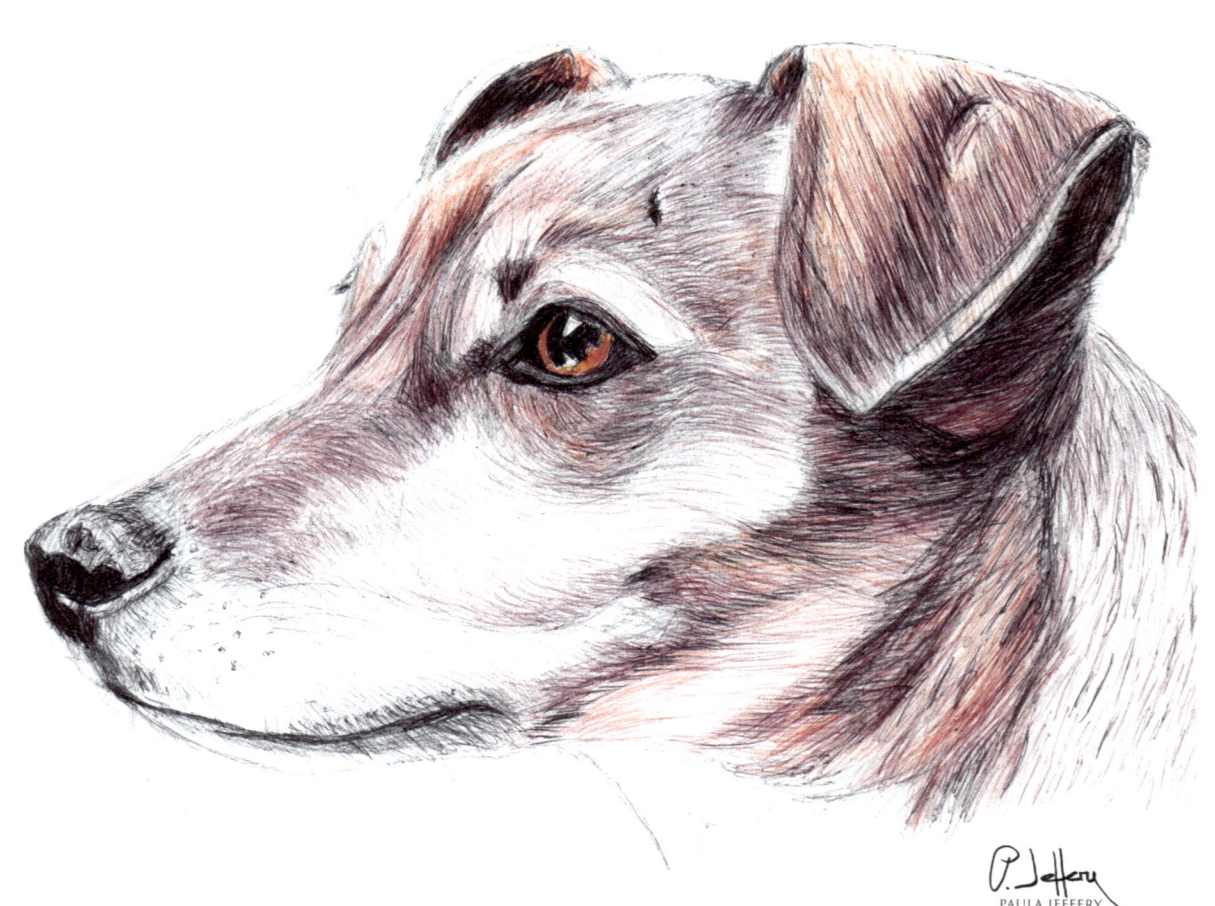

PAULA JEFFERY

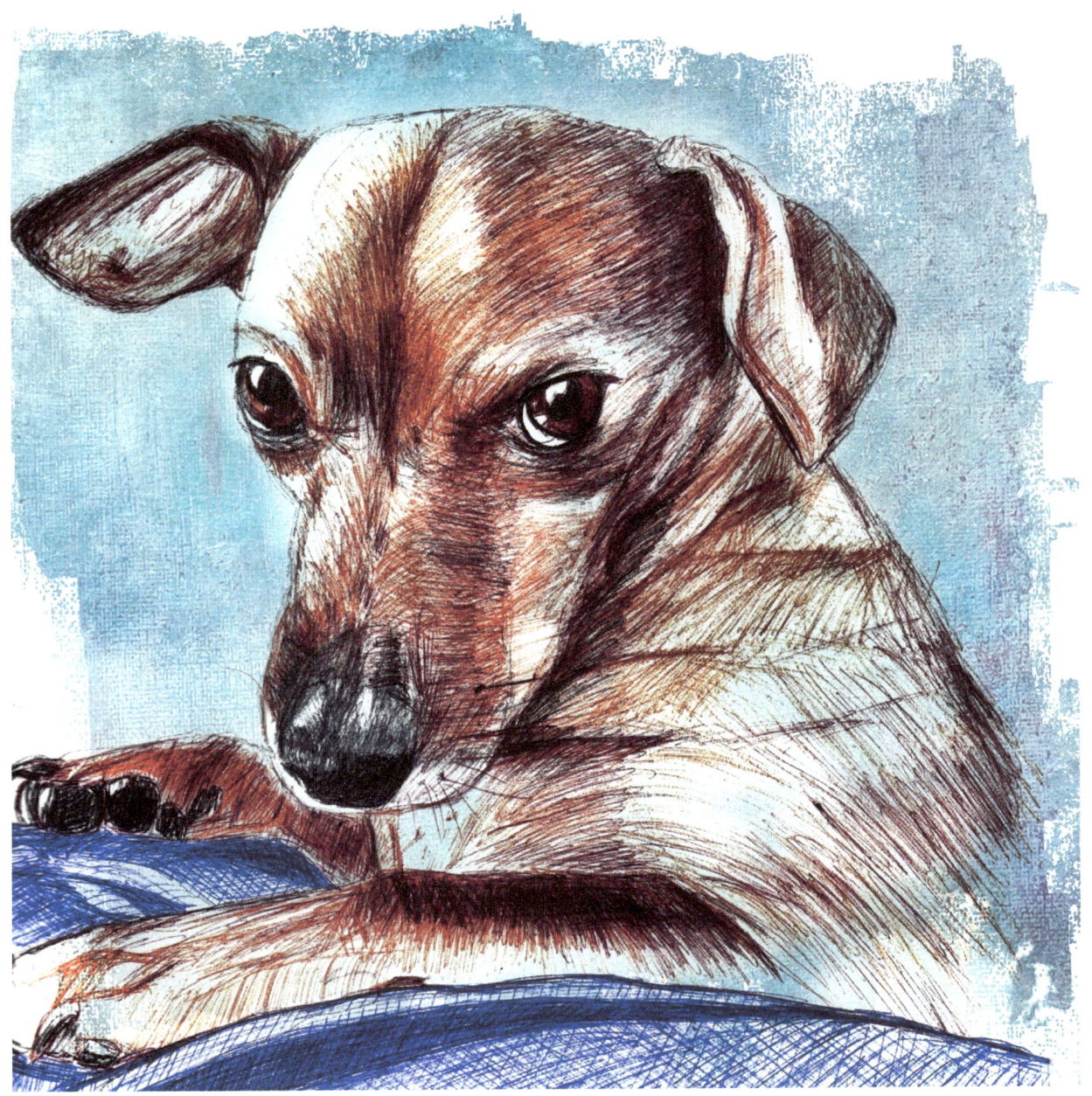

Buck: Kimberly Taylor

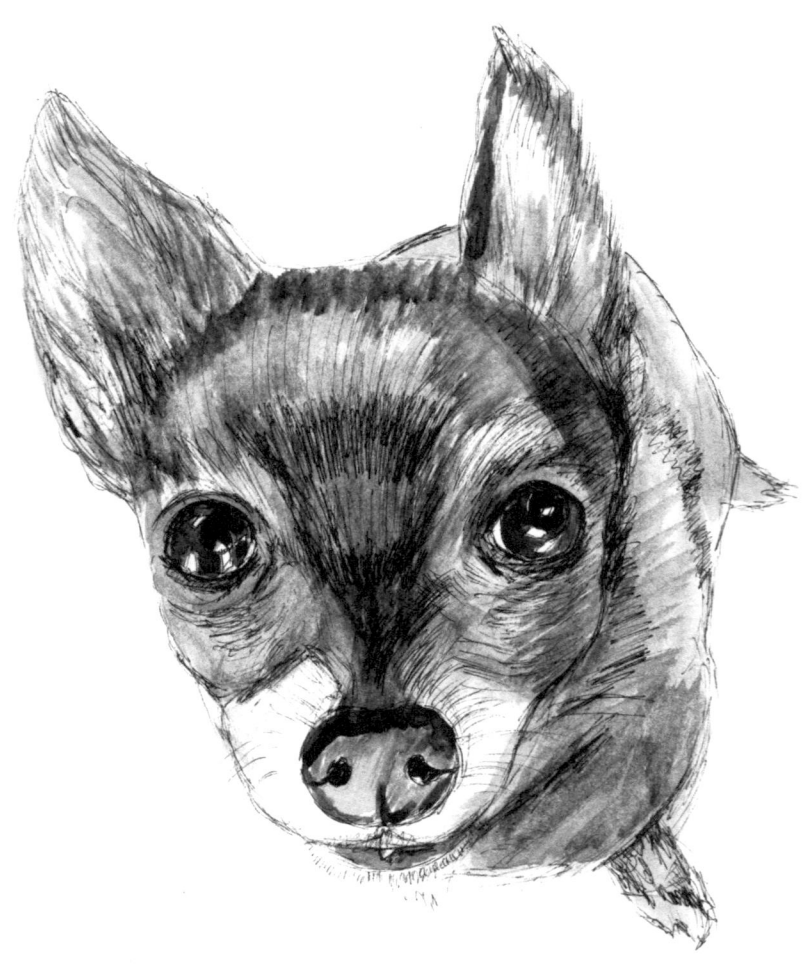

Louis: Kimberly Taylor

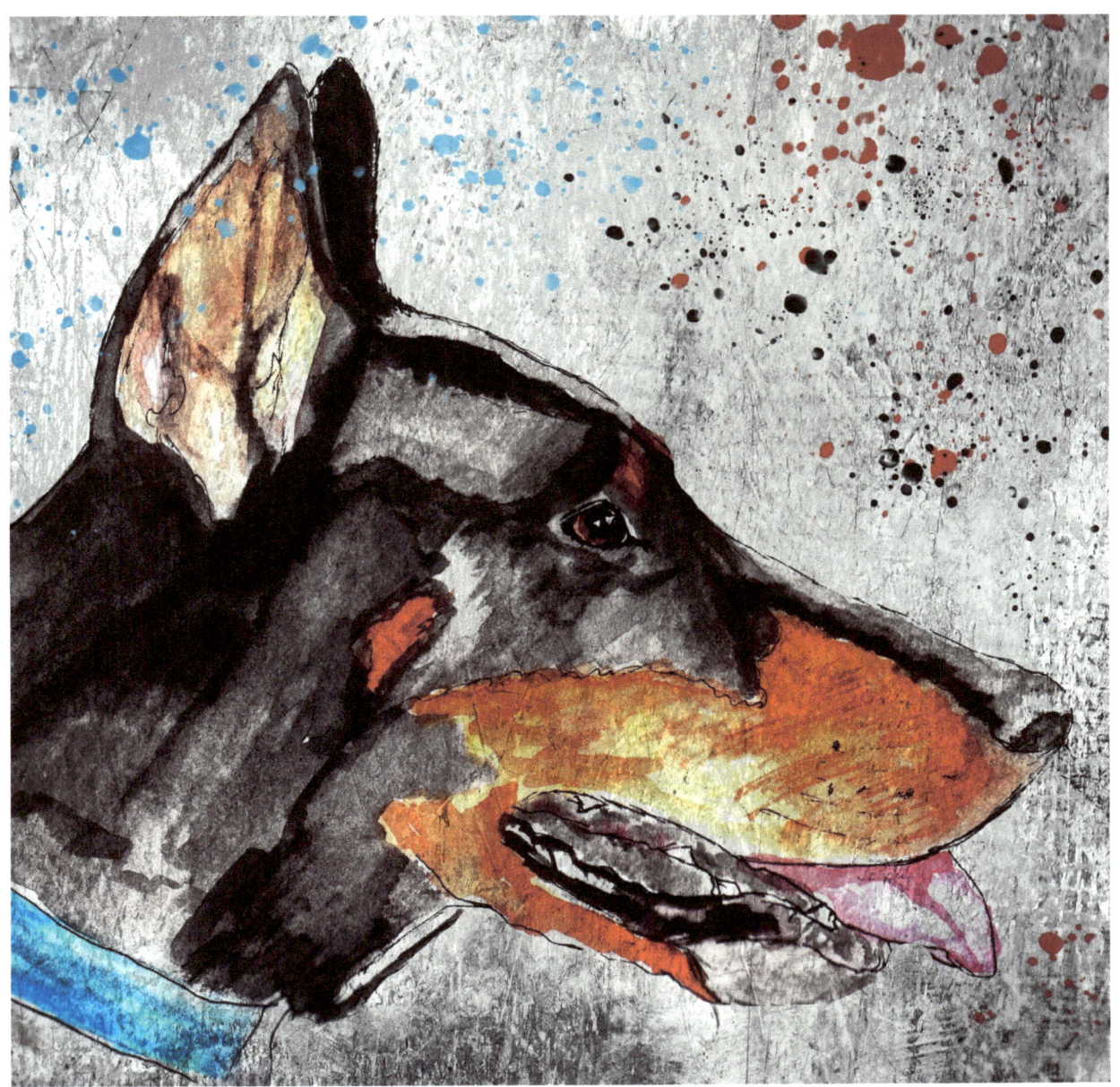

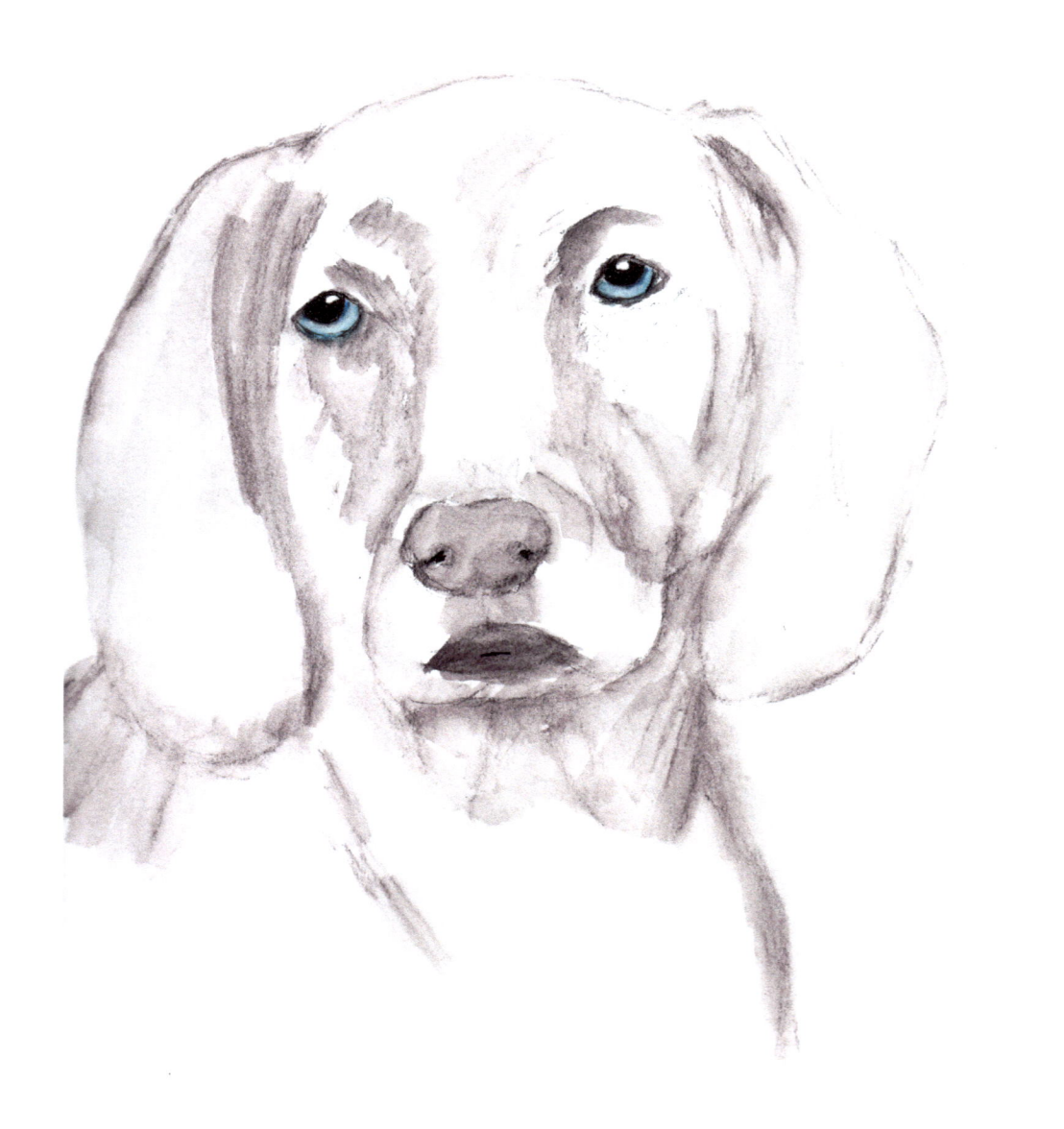

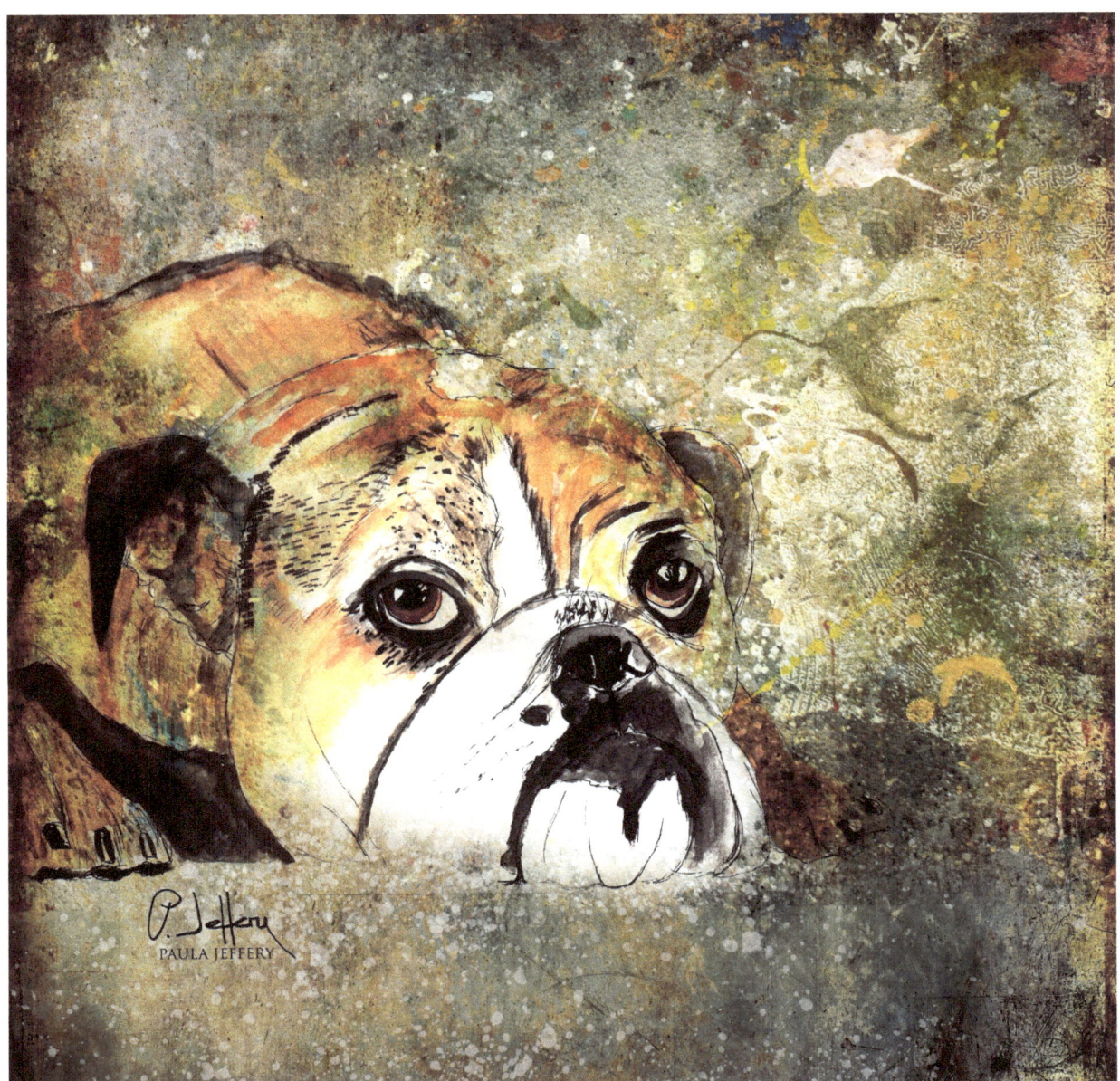

PAULA JEFFERY